Power of the Enneagram:

How to Understand Your Personality Type Better So You Can Use It to Your Advantage.

(Includes a Test for the 9 Personality Types)

Written by: Elena Wright

Elena Wright © Copyright 2020 - All rights reserved.

The content contained within this book may not be reproduced, duplicated or transmitted without direct written permission from the author or the publisher.

Under no circumstances will any blame or legal responsibility be held against the publisher, or author, for any damages, reparation, or monetary loss due to the information contained within this book, either directly or indirectly.

Legal Notice:

This book is copyright protected. It is only for personal use. You cannot amend, distribute, sell, use, quote or paraphrase any part, or the content within this book, without the consent of the author or publisher.

Disclaimer Notice:

Please note the information contained within this document is for educational and entertainment purposes only. All effort has been executed to present accurate, up to date, reliable, complete information. No warranties of any kind are declared or implied. Readers acknowledge that the author is not engaging in the rendering of legal, financial, medical or professional advice. The content within this book has been derived from various sources. Please consult a licensed professional before attempting any techniques outlined in this book.

By reading this document, the reader agrees that under no circumstances is the author responsible for any losses, direct or indirect, that are incurred as a result of the use of information contained within this document, including, but not limited to, errors, omissions, or inaccuracies.

Table of Contents

Introduction 9
    But what is it exactly and how can it help me improve my life?....12
    What should I do now?..23

The Quiz 25

Chapter 1 – The History of Enneagram and
How to Take Advantage.. 35
    The Early Origins of the Enneagram 36
    The Modern Origins of the Enneagram 37
    How can we use our personality type to our advantage? 39
    What should I do next? 41

Chapter 2 – Type One: The Reformer 45
    Introduction to *The Reformer:* 46
    PROFILE: *The Reformer* 47
    How *The Reformer* can hack their own success? 49
    Using the enneagram to achieve self-improvement 50
    Strengthening Relationships – tapping into your own strengths 53
    Achieving your career potential 54
    Master your finances by honing your skills 57
    Build emotional, mental, and physical health practices that work best for *The Reformer* 60
    Become a Leadership Rockstar with your enneagram skillset 62
    Top Tips to Boost your efficiency through problem-solving methods that work for you 63
    Discover a path to spirituality that works best for your personality type 65
    Connect the dots to create a vision for progress and growth..65

Affirmations for *The Reformer* 70

Chapter 3 – Type Two: The Helper 71

Introduction to *The Helper:* 72
PROFILE: *The Helper* 73
How *The Helper* can hack their own success? 75
Using the enneagram to achieve self-improvement 77
Strengthening Relationships – tapping into your own strengths 78
Achieving your career potential 84
Master your finances by honing your skills 86
Build emotional, mental, and physical health practices that work best for *The Helper* 89
Become a Leadership Rockstar with your enneagram skillset ...92
Top Tips to Boost your efficiency through problem-solving methods that work for you 93
Discover a path to spirituality that works best for your personality type 95
Connect the dots to create a vision for progress and growth ..96
Affirmations for *The Helper* 100

Chapter 4 – Type Three: The Achiever   101

Introduction to *The Achiever:* 102
PROFILE: *The Achiever* 102
How *The Achiever* can hack their own success? 105
Using the enneagram to achieve self-improvement 108
Strengthening Relationships – tapping into your own strengths ...110
Achieving your career potential 113
Master your finances by honing your skills 116
Build emotional, mental, and physical health practices that work best for *The Achiever* 118
Become a Leadership Rockstar with your Enneagram skillset ..121

Top Tips to Boost your efficiency through problem-solving
methods that work for you 124
Discover a path to spirituality that works best for your personality type ..126
Connect the dots to create a vision for progress and growth 128
Affirmations for *The Achiever* 133

Chapter 5 – Type Four: The Individualist 135

Introduction to *The Individualist:* 136
PROFILE: *The Individualist* 136
How *The Individualist* can hack their own success? 139
Using the enneagram to achieve self-improvement 142
Strengthening Relationships – tapping into your own strengths ...144
Achieving your career potential 146
Master your finances by honing your skills 149
Build emotional, mental, and physical health practices that
work best for *The Individualist* 151
Become a Leadership Rockstar with your enneagram skillset ...153
Top Tips to Boost your efficiency through problem-solving
methods that work for you 156
Discover a path to spirituality that works best for your personality type.. 159
Connect the dots to create a vision for progress and growth ...161
Affirmations for *The Individualist* 166

Chapter 6 – Type Five: The Investigator 167

Introduction to *The Investigator:* 168
PROFILE: *The Investigator* 169
How *The Investigator* can hack their own success? 171
Using the enneagram to achieve self-improvement 174
Strengthening Relationships – tapping into your own strengths..175
Achieving your career potential 178

Master your finances by honing your skills 180
Build emotional, mental, and physical health practices that work best for *The Investigator* 181
Become a Leadership Rockstar with your enneagram skillset .. 184
Top Tips to Boost your efficiency through problem-solving methods that work for you 186
Discover a path to spirituality that works best for your personality type .. 189
Connect the dots to create a vision for progress and growth ... 190
Affirmations for *The Investigator* 195

Chapter 7 – Type Six: The Loyalist 197

Introduction to *The Loyalist:* 198
PROFILE: *The Loyalist* 199
How *The Loyalist* can hack their own success? 201
Using the enneagram to achieve self-improvement 204
Strengthening Relationships – tapping into your own strengths ... 206
Achieving your career potential 209
Master your finances by honing your skills 212
Build emotional, mental, and physical health practices that work best for *The Loyalist* 214
Become a Leadership Rockstar with your enneagram skillset .. 217
Top Tips to Boost your efficiency through problem-solving methods that work for you 220
Discover a path to spirituality that works best for your personality type .. 222
Connect the dots to create a vision for progress and growth ... 224
Affirmations for *The Loyalist* 228

Chapter 8 – Type Seven: The Enthusiast   229

Introduction to *The Enthusiast:* 230
PROFILE: *The Enthusiast* 230

How *The Enthusiast* can hack their own success? 233
Using the enneagram to achieve self-improvement 235
Strengthening Relationships – tapping into your own strengths..237
Achieving your career potential 240
Master your finances by honing your skills 242
Build emotional, mental, and physical health practices that work best for *The Enthusiast* 243
Become a Leadership Rockstar with your enneagram skillset ..246
Top Tips to Boost your efficiency through problem-solving methods that work for you 248
Discover a path to spirituality that works best for your personality type ..250
Connect the dots to create a vision for progress and growth ...253
Affirmations for *The Enthusiast* 257

Chapter 9 – Type Eight: The Challenger 259

Introduction to *The Challenger:* 260
PROFILE: *The Challenger*..261
How *The Challenger* can hack their own success? 263
Using the enneagram to achieve self-improvement 265
Strengthening Relationships – tapping into your own strengths..267
Achieving your career potential 269
Master your finances by honing your skills 272
Build emotional, mental, and physical health practices that work best for *The Challenger* 274
Become a Leadership Rockstar with your enneagram skillset ..276
Top Tips to Boost your efficiency through problem-solving methods that work for you 278
Discover a path to spirituality that works best for your personality type ..280
Connect the dots to create a vision for progress and growth ...282
Affirmations for *The Challenger* 286

Chapter 10 – Type Nine: The Peacemaker.....287
    Introduction to *The Peacemaker:* 288
    PROFILE: *The Peacemaker* 288
    How *The Peacemaker* can hack their own success? 291
    Using the enneagram to achieve self-improvement 293
    Strengthening Relationships – tapping into your own strengths...295
    Achieving your career potential 297
    Master your finances by honing your skills 300
    Build emotional, mental, and physical health practices that work best for *The Peacemaker*..302
    Become a Leadership Rockstar with your enneagram skillset ..304
    Top Tips to Boost your efficiency through problem-solving methods that work for you 305
    Discover a path to spirituality that works best for your personality type...307
    Connect the dots to create a vision for progress and growth 308
    Affirmations for *The Peacemaker* 313

Conclusion 315

Reference List 320

Introduction

Have you ever wondered why you act in a particular way? Our actions, emotions and cognitions are closely linked, and they form something you'll be familiar with – our personality. Many people wonder how our personality is formed and developed? There are certain characteristics and traits we adopt that make up our personality style, but often the personality that the world sees is the part you show on the outside. When we talk about how our personality is shaped, I'm not simply referring to being happy or moody in particular, but a variety of different things that form our personality.

Our personality is formed as a method of protection to protect us from harm or pain; therefore, our personality protects who we are within and sometimes it's dangerous in that it can hide the real us.

From the moment we are born, it becomes our nature to protect ourselves. It's human nature, as we feel compelled to survive. We sometimes trust others and if this trust is broken, we change our personality. It then becomes more difficult for us to trust but we may not necessarily know why. That's because our personality is linked to our emotions, and it can impact how we think or act.

The Enneagram is a model that categorizes personalities and it recognizes how our personality can help us hide who we really are. By understanding this, we can learn when we should be true to ourselves, and we can use our personality type to our advantage. The Enneagram is a typology and it suggests that there are nine types of personalities. This isn't to suggest that we act in the exact same way as others, as we are all different, but it does help us to understand the way we think, act and feel.

Our personality is individual to us and we often assess the personality of others and decide whether or not we like them. Our own personality is used to attract people and we can feel attracted to others based on their personality, or in reverse, we can repel them. When using the word 'attract', this isn't necessarily of the intimate kind, but it can affect many relationships in our lives, and it can also impact our career too. *Have you ever met someone for the first time and just known that you're going to be good friends because of your connection?* This is because of how we attract or feel drawn to others based on our personality.

The Enneagram can help us to identify the difference between our inner personality and the personality we use as armour. It does this by helping us monitor the different patterns that occur in our personality. As we become more aware of our personality patterns, the more we can understand it and alter or tweak it. We can then use it to make positive changes and this will help us grow and develop emotionally. It can also help us to identify our own personal needs.

Are you ready to start identifying your positive personality traits and negative personality traits, and start using them to lead a fuller life? Well, the Enneagram model can help you get that balance you need for a healthy personality!

But what is it exactly and how can it help me improve my life?

While nobody else in the world acts like us, we often adopt certain traits and characteristics that are similar to our family members. When you figure out your basic/dominant personality, you can be safe in the knowledge of knowing that this doesn't change. Still, the Enneagram takes both a spiritual and psychological perspective. It considers different kinds of feelings, perhaps holy ones, like hope for instance, and it also explores some more negative ones like resentment. The nine personalities are different as they look at the fears, temptations, virtue, and passions of our personality and the dynamics that brings.

To really understand the Enneagram system, you need to learn how it works. To start, take a look at the picture of the Enneagram model and the nine different personalities.

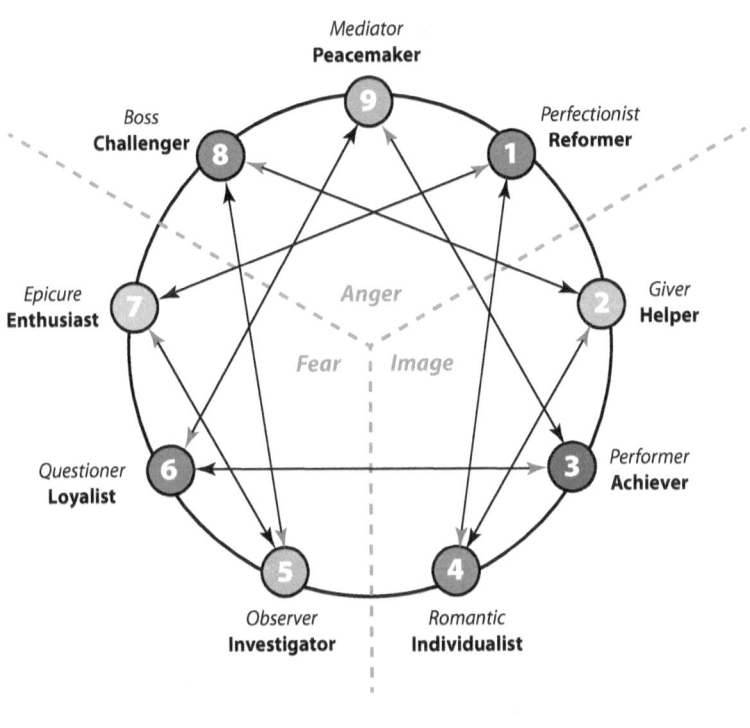

The Enneagram consists firstly of the basic personality types and you must identify your main personality type – the one that best describes you mostly:

1. **The Reformer** – This person is principled and determined to live a purposeful life. They have self-control, but they can also be a perfectionist.

2. **The Helper** – This person is a people-pleaser, but they are also very generous. They can also be possessive, but they regularly display their affection and emotion.

3. **The Achiever** – This person is very driven, and often excel, but they can also be image conscious too. They are adaptable and therefore manage change well.

4. **The Individualist** – This person is very creative and expressive, but they can be dramatic and temperamental too. Sometimes, this person can be self-absorbed.

5. **The Investigator** – An investigator is often a private person, who can sometimes isolate themselves and be extremely secretive to an unhealthy level. On the

plus side, a person who has this type of personality is often innovative and perceptive.

6. **The Loyalist** – This person is often a very engaging person to be around, but they are also suspicious and anxious. Another positive trait is their sense of responsibility and they take this seriously.

7. **The Enthusiast** – An enthusiast can be spontaneous, which makes them exciting people. Although they are scattered at times and disorganized, they are acquisitive and very concerned with getting possessions to prove themselves, but they are also versatile and flexible.

8. **The Challenger** – This person is highly confident. They walk into the room, and they make an impact. They are decisive and willful; yet sometimes they can come across as being very confrontational, which can sometimes feel intimidating.

9. **The Peacemaker** – The peacemaker is very reassuring and receptive. They are sometimes complacent, resigned and therefore they are good at tolerating others.

Levels of Development – There are different development levels with the Enneagram model within its internal structure. This covers attitudes, motivations, behaviors and defenses which are shaped by the nine personality types. The levels of development focus on healthy, average and unhealthy usage of each personality trait, and it focuses on a psychological shift. Levels 1-3 are healthy. Liberation, psychological capacity and social value are all part of the healthy level of development. The imbalance or social role, interpersonal control, and overcompensation can be average, and they are levels 4-6. Unhealthy levels are 7-9, and they include violation, obsession and compulsion, and pathological destructiveness. It's important to lose these higher levels and ensure that we are moving down the levels and towards healthiness.

Throughout this book, we will be concentrating on these nine personality types and the levels of development. This book is a starting block, an introduction to the Enneagram. There is so much more to the Enneagram and although you can start with this book, it isn't the end. It's not always as simple as finding one personality type, as we are all different and can display elements of several types. Once you know your dominant personality type, you can explore further by looking at the centers and the wings, but your dominant personality type will always remain the same. This is your key anchor point in the Enneagram. The Enneagram Institute is a great online resource if you want to explore your personality type further. We've touched on centers and wings below, so you know what to expect.

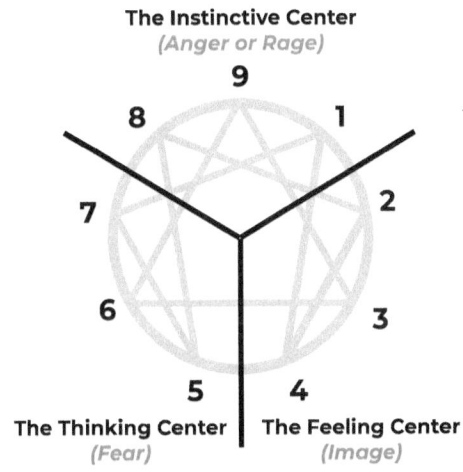

The Centers – Nobody has one personality type, but one will be the most dominant. This dominant personality then links to the center and each center is attached to a dominant emotion. The emotions that run across the center of the Enneagram model above are: anger or rage, image or shame, and fear. The emotions are attached to one of the three centers of each personality. Centers are categories that link commonalities between the three personality types in each group. At the top, we have the instinctive center (anger), to the left we have the thinking center (fear) and to the right we have the feeling center (image). Each center stretches over three personality types. 2, 3, and 4 belong to the image center, 5, 6, and 7 belong to the fear center, and 8, 9, and 1 belong to the instinctive center. That's because each center is closely linked to three personalities in the model. The centers are distinguished by the commonalities between the three personality types in their group share, especially in the way they manage their emotions. As an example, *Eights, Nines,* and *Ones* all have anger, but while Eights might act out their anger and act on instincts, Nines are more likely to deny their anger and ignore their instincts. Ones, on the other hand, tend to try to repress them both (Enneagram Institute, 2020)[i]. For a more in depth analysis of your centers and instincts along with their subtypes, you can pay for the in-depth, online test available with the Enneagram Institute.

The Wing – Most people are a unique mix of personalities and although one of them is the most prominent, one of the two types adjacent to this on the Enneagram circumference is called your wing. Your wing represents another side to your personality and sometimes this is contradictory to your prominent type. Human beings and the way they think, act and feel are very complex, so your wing is a kind of secondary element that helps you to develop a stronger understanding of your personality. *Have you ever felt that you couldn't make your mind up?* First you like something, and then you don't... You then feel unsure as to whether you do or not. Well our personality can be just as indecisive and sometimes we do disagree with ourselves. Some people even claim to have a 2-wing personality, giving them a mix of three personality types from the Enneagram model.

The whole idea of the Enneagram is based around the fact that although you have a dominant personality type, nobody fits one personality type exactly. This is why each personality has wing possibilities that indicate how you are different from your dominant personality type. When it comes to wings, online Enneagram tests are not always 100% accurate, so the best way to find out your wing is to study the Enneagram personality types in detail and determine which is more like you. If you do this, it's important to be honest with yourself. We'll talk more about wings in the relevant chapters and help you determine your wing/s (A Quick Guide To Wings In Enneagram - Innercle.com, 2020)[ii].

Direction of Disintegration (Stress) and Direction of Integration (Growth) – We know already that our personality type is not stagnant as we or on a constant journey of change. Our personality type follows inner lines within the Enneagram, and this is when we start to dip into the different personality types. The Direction of Disintegration and Integration are both linked to the levels of development that we discussed earlier.

The Direction of Disintegration (Stress)
1-4-2-8-5-7-1
9-6-3-9

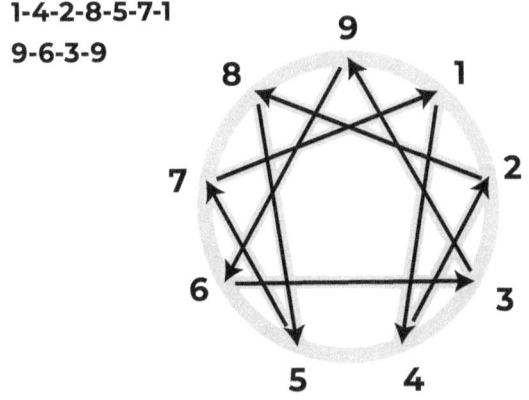

The Direction of Disintegration - is indicated in a number sequence on the Enneagram and this is 1-4-2-8-5-7-1 and 9-6-3-9. This means if your dominant personality is 1, an average 1 headed in the Direction of Disintegration, it would become an unhealthy 4, and an average 4 would become an unhealthy 2, and an average 2 would become an unhealthy 8 and so on. If you are dominant personality 9, 6 or 3, an average 9 would become a 6 under stress (Direction of Disintegration), an average 6 would become an unhealthy 3, and an average 3 would become an unhealthy 9.

The Direction of Integration (Growth)
1-7-5-8-2-4-1
9-3-6-9

The Direction of Integration - is our growth path, as we head towards the healthier levels. It is the opposite of disintegration, but the sequence stays the same as disintegration, but it travels in the other direction – it's basically in reverse. The Direction of Integration is: 1-7-5-8-2-4-1 and 9-3-6-9. Therefore, a an average 1, may be an unhealthy 4 during disintegration, but it's a healthy 7 when it travels in the Direction of Integration. An average 7 becomes a healthy 5, an average 5 becomes a healthy 8, and an average 8 becomes a healthy 2, and an average 4 becomes a healthy 1. Again, if we look at an average 9, it becomes a 3, an average 3 becomes a healthy 6, and an average 6 becomes a healthy 9.

You can read about the Direction of Integration and Direction of Disintegration in each chapter of this book. With the Enneagram model, there is the opportunity to monitor growth and stress, and assess your own levels. You will be able to explore this further in the next chapter, when you complete the personality test and assess your personality as well as the direction you take (The Enneagram Institute, 2020)[iii].

What should I do now?

Before you do anything else in this book, you should take the test to find out your enneagram personality type, so you can identify your dominant personality and work from that. This will help you gain a stronger awareness and understanding of yourself and how you think, feel and act. Each chapter of this book focuses on a personality type, and you can then explore how to use your enneagram to hack your own success, achieve self-improvement, become a leader and improve your skillset, boost your efficiency and creativity, as well as build yourself both physically and mentally. This book will take you on a journey of personal progress and growth and teach you how to connect the dots. In return, you can strengthen your own relationships, reach for your career potential and master your finances.

Sounds too good to be true, right?

Well, you can do this, all through the power of the Enneagram!

It's time to take your personality, nurture it, understand it and use it to your advantage. *Are you ready to grab what you want in life with both hands?*

Good! Because it's time to introduce yourself to your own personality and we'll start with the quiz. You can take control of your life and discover the real you with the power of the Enneagram. Even if you think you already know who you are, your path of self-discovery may surprise you. Things aren't always what they seem, but once we develop an understanding, we have the advantage.

It's time to unleash the power of the Enneagram!

The Enneagram Quiz

Follow the Enneagram quiz to find out your dominant personality. You will be asked to choose from a series of statements or asked questions, and you should answer them as honestly as possible. This will help you to identify your dominant personality, but remember, everyone is different so if the statements or answers don't exactly match, make sure you choose the one that suits you the most.

1. Which of the following statements below best describes you?

    a. I am fair, balanced and principled. I like to get things right and put my best efforts into everything I do.
    b. I appreciate life and others. I care about others and live to support them.
    c. I am confident and driven. I am flexible and always look for the solution.
    d. I am aware and responsive to my own feelings and the feelings of others, but I'm also expressive and creative.
    e. I am a forward-thinker, with good intuition.
    f. I am sensible and I'm committed. I like to feel safe

and secure.
- g. I am fun and do things unexpectedly. I enjoy keeping busy.
- h. I am extremely self-confident and like to lead the way.
- i. I am easygoing. I often agree with others to keep the peace.

2. Are you…

   a. Rational.
   b. Generous.
   c. Pragmatic.
   d. Sensitive.
   e. Innovative.
   f. Engaging.
   g. Spontaneous.
   h. Powerful.
   i. Agreeable.

3. Choose from the sentences below. The chances are you 'won't like' any of the statements or events but choose the one that you dislike the most about your own personality. Complete the sentence: I don't like:

   a. Losing control of my thoughts and feelings.
   b. Not feeling needed. I like being depended upon.

c. Feeling like I've failed. I like to succeed at everything.
d. It when others don't agree with me. I'm sensitive that way.
e. Feeling alone, but sometimes I isolate myself.
f. Feeling insecure or unsafe, as it makes me feel anxious.
g. It when I'm easily distracted as it causes me to be a scatterbrain.
h. It when I'm confrontational in order to get my point across. This happens sometimes when I believe strongly in something that is dismissed by others.
i. That I'm so easy going, it leads to me being complacent.

4. Choose from the statements below:

a. I am a great thinker and I'm great at rationalizing problems to come up with a solution.
b. I do a lot for others and feel that I should get recognition for this.
c. Image is important to me. I like to look my best.
d. I'm sometimes dramatic and temperamental.
e. I can be secretive because I don't like others to know everything and I don't always like to burden others with problems.
f. I get suspicious of others and find it difficult to trust.

g. I can be forgetful. Sometimes I get absorbed or distracted by one thing and forget about another.
h. I am strong-willed and I'm not afraid to go and get what I want.
i. I will do anything for a peaceful life and often just go along with what others decide or want.

5. When it comes to relationships (professional, loving, personal) with others, I'm:

   a. I believe in equality and conventional relationships. I always treat others with respect.
   b. In a relationship, I like to feel valued and needed.
   c. I sometimes like to take the lead in a relationship however, I still think a healthy balance is important.
   d. I think it's important for form special bonds when it comes to relationships.
   e. In a relationship my independence is very important to me. I believe in respect and boundaries.
   f. Trust is important to me in a relationship and I find banter and intellect stimulating.
   g. I look for fun, high-energy relationships and I believe both parties should be thoughtful of one-another.
   h. I tend to look for passionate relationships that will lead somewhere as I like to make things happen.
   i. I enjoy generous and steady relationships that are

natural, and undemanding.

6. Choose the statement that applies to you the most. My career is...

   a. Important to me because it means something. I strive to be the best I can be.
   b. At its best when I help, please and support others.
   c. Keeps me motivated - I'll never stop aiming high and achieving.
   d. Best when I'm using my creativity and although I can work in a team, I enjoy working alone.
   e. Something I think about and want to make a success of. I like a job that challenges me and enables me to unleash innovation.
   f. Something that I'm committed to. I'm very focused and an excellent problem-solver.
   g. I don't take life too seriously, but I work best when I'm kept busy and I enjoy creative roles.
   h. A constant steppingstone as I work my way up the career ladder. I'm a confident leader and decision maker.
   i. Enjoyable. I am great at mediating and solving problems.

7. Choose from the statements below:

a. I like to follow the rules and believe in etiquette.
b. I feel compelled to help others, whether I want to or not.
c. I like to have indications of how I'm doing, in comparison to others.
d. My mind is often critical of both myself and others.
e. I don't like to tell people everything and can be quite secretive or self-absorbed.
f. I often feel worried and doubt others.
g. I like almost everyone I meet.
h. I'm assertive but others have told me that this sometimes comes across as being aggressive.
i. I usually let others take the initiative, rather than acting on my own initiative.

8. When it comes to my appearance:

    a. I like to look well-groomed and smart.
    b. I like to feel comfortable and natural.
    c. I'm image conscious, but dress well and in a professional way.
    d. I go with however I feel, when it comes to my appearance. I have my own style.
    e. I don't like to stand out, so I tend to go for darker or neutral colors when I choose clothes or makeup.
    f. I'm comfortable with my looks and I'm quite a casual

dresser but I dress for the occasion ahead.

g. I love to experiment and have fun with my appearance. I have my own style and don't take things too seriously.

h. I like to look powerful – I like the best clothes, shoes and bags. I also like to be pampered, to relieve stresses.

i. I'm pretty easy going when it comes to my appearance and don't really have preferences.

9. Which statement below most resonates with your beliefs:

a. We must follow the rules and laws, as without them, people wouldn't behave in the right way.

b. Sometimes, I feel like so many people rely on me. It becomes overwhelming but I cope. I have to.

c. My successful image is important to me.

d. Theatre and creativity are my passion, but open mic nights are more my thing so I can perform alone.

e. At times, I'm a loner, but that's not necessarily a bad thing.

f. Sometimes I struggle expressing my feelings, because I tend not to get too involved with them. I just take each day as it comes.

g. When did I grow up? Sometimes I think my inner child is still living its life.

    h. I can't help myself. I can be compulsively honest, and most people find this upsetting.
    i. I don't get stressed out and believe that there are very few urgent things in life. I tend to put things off until tomorrow if I possibly can.

10. What is your biggest fear?

    a. I fear breaking rules and corruption.
    b. I fear being unwanted.
    c. fear being worthless.
    d. fear having no purpose or significance.
    e. I fear helplessness.
    f. fear having no support or guidance.
    g. I fear missing out, being deprived, and being in pain.
    h. I fear others trying to control me.
    i. I fear separation and loss.

BEFORE you go any further, you should know what steps you need to take next. You should collate your results and then before you head to the relevant Enneagram chapter based on your results below, you should read Chapter 1 – The History of Enneagram and How to Take Advantage as this is relevant to anyone.

Remember, this is a basic 10-question quiz to help you decide on your dominant personality. If you want a more detailed quiz you can pay for an enhanced Enneagram quiz through the Enneagram Institute. This can give you more information on your wings and centers. For the purpose of this book, the 10-question quiz should be enough for you to identify your dominant personality.

Check out your results below, so you can start using your personality to your advantage:

Mostly A's – if you chose mostly A's then you are *The Reformer*, and you should check out chapter 2.

Mostly B's – if you chose mostly B's then you are *The Helper*, and you should check out chapter 3.

Mostly C's – if you choose mostly C's then you are *The Achiever*, and you should check out chapter 4.

Mostly D's – if you chose mostly D's then you are *The Individualist*, and you should check out chapter 5.

Mostly E's – if you chose mostly E's then you are *The Investigator*, and you should check out chapter 6.

Mostly F's – if you chose mostly F's then you are *The Loyalist*, and you should check out chapter 7.

Mostly G's – if you chose mostly G's then you are *The Enthusiast*, and you should check out chapter 8.

Mostly H's – if you chose mostly H's then you are *The Challenger*, and you should check out chapter 9.

Mostly I's – if you chose mostly I's then you are *The Peacemaker*, and you should check out chapter 10.

Don't forget to head to chapter 1 next, before you head to your Enneagram personality type chapter!

Chapter 1

The History of Enneagram and How to Take Advantage

The Enneagram model and idea is not a new concept, yet, its popularity is growing. As human beings, we are curious, and we like to explain and understand both the mind and body. *Have you ever wanted to understand your own personality?* When we understand something, we are able to use it to its full potential. It gives us a chance to make changes or develop ourselves, and we all love to self-improve. If we are going to start to understand the idea of the Enneagram, it's important to start at the beginning. Although it is thought to have early origins, not much else is known, but it does have interesting links that can help us to unpick how the Enneagram has developed over time.

The Early Origins of the Enneagram

The initial roots of the Enneagram are unclear. There are suggestions that it has Greek roots, but there are also suggestion linking it to early Christianity, although it has strong Sufi roots too. Spiritual and oral links have been made to the Evagrius' catalogue and the seven deadly sins from Christianity. There are also suggestions that it's embedded into the branches of the Tree of Life in the Kabbalah, in esoteric Judaism. It has also been linked to the Naqshbandi Order, which is a Sufi tradition as the symbol is said to appear in this tradition.

Due to the symbol itself, the Enneagram has been connected to both mathematical and philosophical traditions too. *You may have previously heard of the mathematician Pythagoras?* Well, many people believe the enneagram is linked to his geometry theories. There are also suggestions related to philosophers Plotinus and Ramon Llull, and Jesuit Mathematician Athanasius Kircher (Cloete, 2020)[iv]. We can get to the core of enneagram by exploring its modern origins.

The Modern Origins of the Enneagram

The Enneagram has evolved and been used throughout the 20th and 21st centuries. Over time, its purpose has become much clearer. Oscar Ichazo used the Enneagram of Personality throughout the 1960s' and he used it in his teachings. Chilean psychiatrist, Claudio Naranjo learned the Enneagram from Ichazo and introduced it into the modern psychological world which made this much more widespread. Since this time, various experiments and research has been carried out. There have been many contributions over the years and many psychiatrists have used this, even outside the Enneagram community. It has been used as a framework to help us understand social styles for instance (Cloete, 2020)[v].

All of this information is interesting as the Enneagram is certainly an interesting tool, but you want to know how this Enneagram can be used to help you, right?

The people who've worked on the Enneagram over the years have made some excellent discoveries and that influences how we use the Enneagram today and the power it holds.

The Enneagram is now used as a classification model in psychology and it's used by many psychologists to bring awareness to key unconscious strategies you use to ensure your needs are met. It can help you to observe the mechanics of your personality, which can help with personal growth. We've already been introduced to the diagram itself and the 9 personality types. You may have already noticed that each type has a key stress point and using the positive aspects of your personality can help you to promote a healthier lifestyle with less stress.

But, how can we take advantage of our own personality?

How can we use our personality type to our advantage?

To improve ourselves we have to know what the problem is. *How can we make changes if we don't know what we need to change?* Now, the Enneagram isn't necessarily all about change, it's more about observing and knowing ourselves. The more we know, the higher our awareness and the more empowered we feel, and the more we gain control of our own destiny. It's in your hands!

The Enneagram can help us develop a healthy vision for the future and map out our journey into achieving it, in the best way that works for us. A path for one person, may not be the same path that works for another – that's because we are all different. *We know this, right, this is nothing new!* But sometimes people are surprised that their path is in a different direction. For example, if two people start working at the same time in a junior position and both aspire to become a manager, one may train on the job, complete work-based qualifications, and progress quickly. The other may choose to attend a college course and complete more academic qualifications over a period of time before they train in the position. This is because some people are more confident and prefer a more hands-on approach, whereas others may prefer to build their knowledge and confidence first, then train in the position. They may even both be ready for the promotion at the same time, but they took different paths to get there. That's just because they are different, and they learn in different ways!

The Enneagram helps us map out our vision in such a way that is healthy for us. If we are aware of our traits and stress triggers, we can ensure we play to our strengths and alleviate any stress triggers. We can also use the centers to shape our plan for growth and development too.

Each personality type wants to satisfy your needs and desires, so it forms a certain behavior that motivates us into achieving or getting what we need or want. Sometimes this behavior is referred to as a passion as it's what we constantly strive for and it is the driving force behind our life plans. More often than not, being driven by our passion isn't the best route for us to take and the Enneagram raises awareness of this and allows us to do this in a more positive or healthier way (Art of wellbeing, 2020)[vi].

If we are aware of our personality traits, especially the dominant traits and the thing that drives us the most, we can use this to our advantage by making healthier plans. We can also transform our future plans by reflecting on how our passions rule and motivate us. The more aware we are, the more likely we are to make positive changes that will help us develop and get what we want in life.

What should I do next?

All that's left for you to do is to explore the different personality types and use the Enneagram to work out your dominant and secondary personality types. You can then explore your personality and you can also figure out how to use this, along with your centers and passions for the greater good. You can then use your newly found knowledge and awareness to enable and empower your future. You can also take a healthy and positive stance when planning for your future.

This book reviews all nine personality types in detail, which will help you to understand more about each type of personality and how it might apply your inner personality. As an introductory book, it's the starting block to help you develop and grow using the power of Enneagram.

The Enneagram will help you to create balance when it comes to your intelligences as many theorists suggest that everyone has a primary intelligence, a supporting intelligence and a repressed intelligence that we often block out. There are many reasons why we may choose to repress a center, but this can have a negative reaction as we can suffer fear and anxiety, distress or panic, or we can become angry. With this in mind, we need to identify the intelligence or center we least use. We don't cover the centers in depth in this introductory book, but we do look at the levels of development in detail. If you want to explore your centers further, you will need to do some further research. There is so much more to the Enneagram, so you can dig deeper into your dominant personality, once you know what that is. Theorists say that in order to develop ourselves, we should start utilizing our mind again, through Enneagram, as it will create a healthy rebalance between the centers. In order to do this, we need to know our personalities and work out which of our centers (or intelligences) we have forgotten. We can then use this, so we can operate in a healthy way (Art of wellbeing, 2020)[vii]. Once we understand more about our personality and centers, we can start to include them and make steady improvements.

This book will help you interpret your personality traits and help you create balance by understanding your dominant personality and exploring the healthy, average and unhealthy levels. Remember that in life, we shouldn't constantly muddle through in our comfort zone. To get what we want and grow, we must take a leap and allow ourselves to be exposed. We will explore how you can start to unpick and trust your instincts and build on your self-awareness so that you can embrace your transformation through the power of the Enneagram. You are the master of your own destiny!

If you're ready to start making positive changes, let's figure out your personality and use the Enneagram to your advantage. Let's learn how to manifest ourselves, using the power of the Enneagram.

You should've completed the quiz already, so head to your dominant personality chapter. If you have more than one, then you should look over both and see which one is more like you. This is just the beginning for you, so read through carefully, and you can start to make some positive changes in your life!

Chapter 2

Type One: The Reformer

It's only right to start at personality type one, on the Enneagram. This is known as *The Reformer* because they want to change the world. It is said that they want to make things different and will use their influence to do so which makes them very determined people. *But how do you really know if you're a reformer?*

Introduction to The Reformer:

The Reformer is a person of principle and they are said to be idealistic. They are self-controlled which means they are good at keeping a cool head. They are purposeful, with a strong sense of what's wrong and right. Another positive trait is that they are known to be conscientious and ethical too, but they often feel the need to justify themselves and they find criticisms difficult. Their key motivations are wanting to improve, and they always push for more in everything they do, because they are perfectionists.

The Reformer is often afraid of making mistakes, but they are well-organized. They sometimes resent others and can be impatient (The Enneagram Institute, 2020)[viii].

PROFILE: *The Reformer*

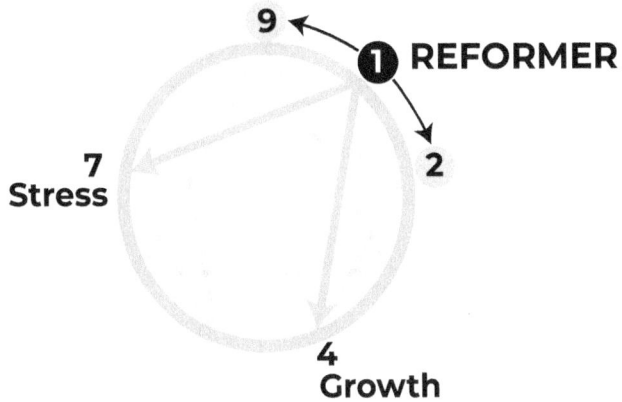

Key Desire: To have integrity, be fair and decent.

Key Fear: They fear being immoral and flawed. These fears stem from perfectionism.

Wings possibilities: If you find that you often isolate yourself and sometimes disconnect from others, then you could have a nine-wing. If you worry a lot about making the wrong choices, you could have a two-wing, and in that case, you are *the Advocate.*

One with a nine-wing: If you are type one, with a nine-wing, you are *The Idealist.* Idealism is something that both type *The Reformer* and *The Peacemaker* personality types have in common.

Your dominant personality is a one, but if you have a nine-wing, it shows you have some traits that link with type nine/*The Peacemaker.* Ones already look for and relate to the ideal, and as the idealism is reinforced by the nine-wing. A one with a nine-wing tends to have idealizations in relation to others and they are often more cerebral. The only point to consider is that ones want to strive for change but a nine, as a subtype, wants to avoid stirring up any conflict (Enneagram Type 1w9 - The Idealist, 2020)[ix].

One with a two-wing: If you are a one and have a two-wing, you are *The Advocate.* You have the natural instinct to be fair and honest and this is fuelled by your dominant personality, but also fuelled by your two-wing. Type two is *The Helper,* so you share some traits with ones, for example, you are sensitive to others, and you strive for social change and justice. You do need to be careful as you can become frustrated with others if you don't get what you want – this is common for both types, so if your secondary personality is a two-wing, be sure to keep this under control (Enneagram Type 1w2 - The

Activist, 2020)[x].

Key motivations: *The Reformer* wants to be right and do better. They are consistent and believe they are above being disparaged.

Strengths: They are a principled, wise, realistic and virtuous.

Stress points and Growth: They can become moody and irrational when their arrow heads to number 4 in their direction of Disintegration (stress). When the arrow moves to number 7 in their direction of Integration (growth), they can change from angry and critical to joyful and spontaneous (The Enneagram Institute, 2020)[xi].

How *The Reformer* can hack their own success?

The Reformer can hack their own success because they are known for their honesty and integrity. Their self-control means that they can handle difficult situations and they are great problem solvers.

The Reformer is strong-willed which means they strive to achieve, and they enjoy teaching others. If they learn to harness their personality and keep it at its healthy level, they can achieve success.

If you're a *Reformer*, you can use your strengths to excel. As a headstrong person who advocates for change. This means that you like to get what you want in life.

You work best with order and you like to have well-structured, systematic plans, so being organised is a strength that will serve you well through life. You also have great creative skills and abilities too which means you can think out of the box, and you're innovative. They are excellent skills to help you succeed in everything you do. As you work best when you plan, you can set goals and objectives as your framework.

Using the enneagram to achieve self-improvement

If you're *The Reformer* there are many things you can do to self-improve. The first thing you should be doing is by finding your weakest center (intelligence) and working out how you can create balance.

If you want to get better at something, the first step is to think about what you really want in life. Spend some time reflecting and focusing on what you want in life. Use your newly found awareness to identify how you can move forward, and as *The Reformer* likes to follow rules and strategies, set some end goals for the future and objectives to help you achieve them.

The Reformer is a perfectionist, and this can hold you back. You can delay work projects, frustrate others, and this can often be seen as a selfish act. Don't worry, this is something you can work on. Here are our top 5 ways to stop being a perfectionist.

1. You need to recognise that you are a perfectionist. When you acknowledge this and become aware, you've taken the first step.
2. The next step is to stop and think. Next time something isn't going your way, stop and assess the situation. Ask yourself questions – *should I seek advice from others? Am I delaying the project? Does everything need to be perfect right now? How can I move forward? What's the best*

outcome and what's the worst?

3. Acceptable, good, and better standards. If you are a perfectionist, you're always going to strive to be better, so set this as your better standard and work backwards. *What's your good standard? What's an acceptable standard?* You can then create goals and there's no harm in striving for the better goal but remember that acceptable is still a win.
4. Retrain the way you think. We are often our own worst enemy, so use the logical skills you have to break down your barriers. Train yourself to accept the 'acceptable' standard as a win and celebrate your achievement. If you find yourself pushing for more, ask yourself *is it necessary? Is it realistic?* The main thing is to take the time to think, rather than acting on impulse.
5. Move on! Especially so when you've achieved your goal and there's nothing more to do. Maybe it's of an acceptable standard but it's met time restraints – that's great! That means it's time to move on. Don't overthink it. Moving on keeps your mind busy, so ensure there is another task

or project for you to move onto, or at least something for you to do, when you've finished. Giving yourself a reason to move on or doing something else, will certainly occupy your mind (May Busch, 2020)[xii].

Strengthening Relationships – tapping into your own strengths

The Reformer likes honesty when it comes to a relationship. They offer this and expect it in return. They are reliable and dedicated to the relationships in their lives, but they do try and avoid or pass the fault or blame, which means if there are issues, or if a relationship breaks down they struggle to admit it's on their part. This can sometimes cause conflict and frustration in personal, professional, private, and sexual relationships.

The Reformer has many positive traits. They are very loyal, and they can use their strengths to strengthen relationships. They need to be honest with themselves and be aware that their perfectionisms and ideals can cause frustration. If you are *The Reformer,* take a step back and assess your own behavior from an outside point of view and don't be afraid to listen. Remember, nobody is faultless and there is more than one person in a relationship. Use your rationale to control your internal defence system and if you want to improve the world, try improving your relationships first.

The Reformer is known to be spontaneous now and then, so if this is your personality type, don't be afraid to surprise others. In a relationship, people tend to just want to spend time with you. Surprise your workmate with their favorite refreshment or spend some quality time with your mother or daughter. If it's private or sexual relationship, why not arrange dinner, out or in. You'll find it much more relaxing if you don't expect anything. Everyone deserves time to kick back, so take some time out (Relationship Type 1 with Type 1 — The Enneagram Institute, 2020)[xiii].

Achieving your career potential

Career prospects are excellent for *The Reformer,* but

they can find this frustrating if things don't go their way. You are ethical, dedicated and reliable, and you also have creative traits. You're a natural teacher, but if you are heading for a high-pressured job, your perfectionism could suggest to your prospective employer that you will struggle to cope in a stressful and pressured environment. If you allow this part of your personality to get the better of you, then it could certainly cause you a lot of stress and anxiety.

If you want to achieve your career potential, you need to get your perfectionism under control. Your need for perfectionism shouldn't cloud your judgement, affect your decisions, or prevent you from meeting deadlines, goals and any other expectations.

We all have a dream career and you should certainly achieve your dreams, and this is how you should strive for yours:

- Use your skills to create some career goals.
- Write a list of skills and qualifications you need for this career type.

- Think of your personal development. What skills do you need to have for this role? Be rational and constructive. Think of what you might need to change and how you can change it.
- Break down your goals into smaller objectives and detail how you will reach your goal.
- Finally, match your findings from the Enneagram to check you're discussing all of your strengths. Consider your weaknesses too and ensure you have a plan to overcome any that may prevent you from succeeding in that career.

Sometimes we have to change aspects of ourselves in a professional capacity, but *The Reformer* has so many skills and traits that they can utilize. They need a job that means something because they live to make improvements. They are organized, honest, and they want to live their life in the right way. They aren't afraid to speak out, but they must learn that nobody is right all of the time, and you must learn to accept constructive criticism for improvement purposes. Especially if you need to study qualifications (Enneagram Type 1 - The Idealist, 2020)[xiv].

Master your finances by honing your skills

As *The Reformer* likes to make improvements, they often set the bar high because their mentality means that everything needs improvements. That means that change is often inevitable as they are often inclined to spend money on anything that means improvement, especially self-improvement.

The idea of perfectionism comes into play here and it is often a downfall when it comes to money. They raise the standard so high, that nothing is ever enough. If they set the goal to save $10,000 when they reach $10,000, it isn't enough, they need to save double that figure and they keep increasing it.

Now, the first thing *The Reformer* needs to do if they want to master their finances is accept that nothing is perfect. They need to be happy with what they have or at least a realistic standard or goal. *When is it enough?* To do this, they can set realistic finance goals and stick to them.

As mentioned above, goals need to be realistic. Many Reformers are renowned for setting high expectations. High expectations are great, but you need to decide *what's good enough?* Things that work are not always perfect, but improvements are not essential. If you buy a new car, it may have plenty of legroom, but it may have very little trunk space.

When managing your finances, *The Reformer* has some fantastic skills. They are honest and reliable, motivated and they want to improve the world. They can make a start by improving their finances, but they need to change the way they think about them. If you have saved $10,000, you should be thinking about the most lucrative savings or investment account you can use. Or in order to save, *what can you cut back on?* For example, if you want to save money fast, you may need to stop buying food brands in your food shopping and try a cheaper brand or store. You can use your desire and the want to improve, to motivate you to achieve your financial goals.

If you are inclined to spend your money on

self-development, don't be sucked in easily. Ensure that this will be of benefit to you and research your product or service. Don't be afraid to note down the pros and cons so that you can assess just how beneficial the spend will be. Do your research, and always take care when spending money on self-development. Shop around and check out other options too. Not everyone is as honest as you!

The thing that must be considered here is that you are the one who sets the standard; therefore, you are the one who pushes for this perfection. You must remember that flaws are natural. If you're looking to save or reduce your spending, there are no perfect suppliers or ways to save or spend. If we use bank accounts for an example, you may not have the highest interest rate, but you may have full access to your funds. You can't always have the best of both.

The skills you need to work on if you want to master your finances is your ability to listen. Take advice from professionals in the bank or a financial advisor, to help you make informed financial decisions. This way you can work out the best option for you. Accept that this may not be perfect but work out what you would accept. A *Reformer* should always celebrate their wins – if you save money, or spend on something you need, that's beneficial, then you should celebrate this.

Build emotional, mental, and physical health practices that work best for *The Reformer*

Learning how to build your emotional, mental and physical health practices is important for anyone, but you can improve your health in line with your personality. If symptoms are extreme, persist or get worse, remember that you should seek advice from a qualified medical professional.

The Reformer often feels stressed and frustrated as a result of their need for perfectionism. To support their emotional and mental health needs, they should find appropriate ways to express their feelings. It's easy to bite the head off the ones we love, but we need to stop any outbursts caused by stress.

The Reformer is known for putting a lot of pressure on themselves, so if you feel emotional or stressed and frustrated, stop yourself from reacting and take some time to reflect. *Ask yourself, why do I feel this way?* Because you may be fully aware of what is causing this. You can also talk through these issues with your family and friends, but if it's deeper than that, you should visit your doctor or enlist the help of a counselor for help and support. This will assist your emotional wellbeing and your mental health.

There are also some exercises that can promote your physical, mental and emotional wellbeing. There's no doubt, that as a *Reformer,* life can be pressurised and stressful, and you need to learn how to relax. There are three exercises suggested below to match your personality:

- Power Walk – go for a brisk stroll and walk off any stress and pressure you feel.
- Tai Chai – Try Tai Chi. There are often classes held in Tai Chi and it's this is a relaxing type of exercise that is great for both the mind and body.

- Yoga – Yoga is extremely possible. Its ability to focus on controlled breathing is a great calming technique for the mind and body. The stretches help you to stay supple and flexible, so yoga is not only good for the mind, but it's good for the body too.

Become a Leadership Rockstar with your Enneagram skillset

The Reformer is an ideal leader. They are great at making decisions and always want to live by rules and do what's right. This person thrives on having a purpose, so they want to be the best at everything they do. This means they can harness this power to motivate others and indicate the high standards and expectations they have for their team. *The Reformer* is a great leader as they strive for equality and want to make a difference. A key skill of a leader is to motivate others, and *The Reformer* is always motivated, as they want to achieve their high standards. They need to learn to use this skill to motivate and encourage others. They are also great problem solvers, have excellent creative skills, and like to take practical action. Due to their strong principles, they are trusted by others.

A leader likes to be in control, but they need to ensure that they aren't too rigid with their team as they would be in danger of repressing them. They must learn to listen to the people who they lead, they should encourage them to share their opinions and they must ensure that their need for perfectionism doesn't cause problems for others. A leader must be open to change, and this must extend to personal development/change too. If you want to become a Leadership Rockstar, you must be willing to make a personal journey of change and ensure you are an understanding leader who can manage stressful and pressurized situations. *The Reformer* is a thinker, who is dedicated to others. There's no doubt that they will put everything into becoming the best leader they can be, but they must lead by example.

Top Tips to Boost your efficiency through problem-solving methods that work for you

1. The first step to problem-solving for *The Reformer* is to be aware of the problem and be able to identify any issues clearly. As their personality naturally gets them to avoid blame and strive to be perfect, identifying problems (especially if they are personal) might not be the easiest. However, it should be noted that this is the most important step.
2. The next step to problem solving is to list your options. You may need or want to involve others at this stage, as sometimes others help us to understand and work-out the best answer.
3. When you have a list, you need to assess your options. *What are the pros and cons?*
4. It's then down to you (and possibly your team, family members or friends) to make an informed decision based on your assessment.

Due to your personality type, you should be prepared to listen to what others think. Ensure you aren't biased when problem solving based on your preference. You can use your thinking skills and your morals to consider the best course of action. *The Reformer* is motivated to solve problems quickly, but be careful that you don't make impulsive decisions, due to your frustrations that stem from your need for perfectionism. Remember, nobody is always right.

Discover a path to spirituality that works best for your personality type

The Reformer needs to learn methods of relaxation, to help them walk a path of spirituality. For this particular personality type, meditation will be ideal if you want to discover spirituality. Start with guided meditations to calm an active mind, and to help change attitudes.

There are apps you can download and websites you can visit to download guided meditations. Take 10-20 minutes, morning and night to target your personality. In the morning, look for guided meditations that help you be happy, satisfied and calm. In the evening, look to calm your mind, deep sleep and instil positivity.

Connect the dots to create a vision for progress and growth

If you think your dominant personality is *The Reformer*, it's time to create your vision for personal growth. This means it's time to explore the levels of development for this personality type.

There are 9 levels of development for each personality type. We all strive for healthy levels (levels 1-3) and as *The Reformer*, who strives for perfection, you'll certainly be aiming to achieve this as you want to be at your best. Average levels (levels 4-6) are acceptable (so please remember this), and if you are at unhealthy levels (levels 7-9) you need to be ready to make a change. Just remember that if you are at unhealthy levels, you can make the leap by making positive changes. Also, be forgiving, because nobody is perfect, and we all have our good times and our bad times. You can look at the level descriptors below and decide where you are right now, and where you want to be.

Healthy levels
Level 1 – This is *The Reformer* at their best. They are wise and realistic. They accept less than perfect and are excellent decision makers, always knowing the best

action to take. They are inspiring and have a strong sense of hope. They are determined when it comes to honesty and integrity.

Level 2 – When at level 2, *The Reformer* is a person of moral values and understand what is right or wrong. They are reasonable and rational by nature. They strive for improvements and are conscientious when it comes to personal growth and career goals.

Level 3 – At level 3, *The Reformer* still lives by their principles. They are objective and strive for truth and justice. They feel responsible for others and feel that they have a higher purpose – to ensure fair and ethical treatment for themselves and others.

Average levels

Level 4 – At level 4, *The Reformer* believes themselves to be some kind of crusader because they feel that achieving the greater good is down to them. They often explain how they think things should be, but they want to improve everything as they feel unhappy with reality.

Level 5 – *The Reformer* at this level fears making mistakes. They are frustrated if their ideals are not orderly and consistent, but they are rigid in their views. They often work too much, but they are orderly and well-organized, and they keep their feelings and impulses in check. They are punctual, yet pedantic and compulsive.

Level 6 – When at level 6, *The Reformer* is often moody and a little angry. They want to do the right thing, but they are highly opinionated and judgemental which often contradicts this. They are highly critical of others, and never satisfied. They are becoming more and more impatient.

Unhealthy levels

Level 7 – *The Reformer* is very self-righteous at this level. They have no flexibility and low tolerance for situations and for others. They believe in absolutes and believe that only they are right, because they know the truth. They rationalize their actions, after making harsh judgements.

Level 8 – At this level, *The Reformer* can become obsessive. They obsess about everything, including other's imperfections and this can make them very anxious. Again, they contradict actions, and become quite hypocritical of what they suggest is the right thing.

Level 9 – This is the lowest level and at level 9, *The Reformer* is very condemning of others. They can even be cruel to people who they think are wrongdoers, and they constantly push people away. This can lead to depression and nervous breakdowns, as well as other mental health issues. It can lead to OCD (Obsessive Compulsive Disorder) or Personality Disorders. Sometimes, people get into highly depressive states and make suicide attempts (The Enneagram Institute, 2020)[xv].

If you have read these levels and feel you are in the unhealthy levels, then you must seek professional medical advice right away. Go and visit your doctor! If you are average or healthy, you can start to plan your path of improvement and personal growth. We've already talked about setting goals and smaller objectives to help you achieve these goals.

If you feel you are already at level 1, you need to maintain your level. Write out a description of 'the best' you and remind yourself every day of who you are. Ensure you stay there. Sometimes, our levels dip or something new happens and improvements are needed.

Affirmations for *The Reformer*

Enough is enough. This is enough and I am enough.

Every path that is not perfect is unique. Unique is better than perfect.

I accept that I'm a work-in-progress.

Chapter 3

Type Two: The Helper

The next enneagram personality type is two, and this is *The Helper*. Are you caring and always looking for ways to help others? If you are, then you could be *The Helper*. Remember that we are concentrating on the dominant personality type, so in order for you to be *The Helper*, your whole personality ethos have to be built around this personality. *So, what personality traits does The Helper have and how do we know if we're The Helper?* Let's find out!

Introduction to *The Helper*:

The Helper is warm-hearted. They are very caring, supportive and nurturing person. They are concerned about the needs, feelings and wants of others, always want to help. *The Helper* is in touch with their own feelings and they are very sincere. They have a huge amount of empathy and are very generous when it comes to giving their time and energy to others, even if this means self-sacrificing on their behalf. Sometimes, *The Helper* is a people-pleaser and they can become needy or possessive as they have a need, to be needed. On occasion, *The Helper* is often unselfish, friendly and loves others unconditionally.

The Helper can get too involved with others, and occasionally they can become a manipulator, because of their need for others to need them. Beneath the surface, they fear being worthless, and often need others to validate the value in themselves. It's important to maintain healthy levels of balance and ensure that if you are *The Helper,* you work on your inner self, and understand your own self-worth (The Enneagram Institute, 2020)[xvi].

PROFILE: *The Helper*

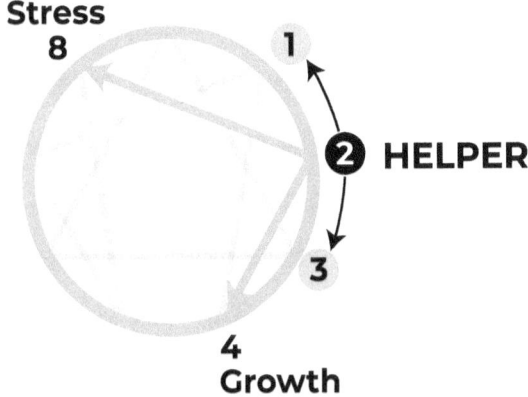

Key Desire: To feel affection and love.

Key Fear: They fear feeling unworthy of love and being unwanted.

Wings possibilities: If you desire acceptance and want to feel worthy, then you could be Enneagram type two with a One-Wing, you're the *Servant.* If you like recognition for your accomplishments and enjoy meeting new people, you could be type two with a three-wing, you're *The Host.*

Two with a one-wing: If you are type two, with a one-wing, you are *The Servant.* Although your dominant personality is *The Helper,* you show traits from type one. You are great at recognizing the needs of others and you're aware of your own growth areas and are great at supporting others (Enneagram Type 2w1 - The Companion, 2020)[xvii].

Two with a three-wing: If you are type two with a three-wing, you are *The Host*. Your personality type shows traits from a type three personality and this means you have a positive attitude and can be quite adaptable when faced with stressful situations (Enneagram Type 2w3 - The Host, 2020)[xviii].

Key motivations: *The Helper* wants to be needed and loved by others. They live to express their feelings for others and want appreciation. They want to quash their own feelings of worthlessness and their own feelings about themselves. If others respond to them, it motivates them further.

Strengths: They are generous, loving and yet extremely humble and deeply unselfish.

Stress points and Growth: *The Helper* can become possessive. When their arrow moves into the direction to number 8 (disintegration), they can become very dominating and sometimes aggressive. When the arrow moves into the direction of integration to number 4, they can be deceptive and often feel a strong sense of pride which can be overpowering. Type Twos can however, become more aware of their emotional state, and can be very self-nurturing (The Enneagram Institute, 2020)[xix].

How *The Helper* can hack their own success?

The Helper can hack their own success by being self-aware. They have so many positive traits that can be used to ensure success, but their own need for self-validation and for being needed can cloud this.

The Helper is very sincere and passionate. They are very interpersonal, well-meaning and driven. As you are driven to help others and have a caring nature, you can excel and lead or coach others.

To be successful, you're going to have to work on yourself. Take yourself on a journey of self-discovery and build up your own self-esteem and self-confidence, so that you know your own worth and value yourself. It's really important that *The Helper* maintains healthy levels of balance by getting to know their own personality.

The Helper works best with others, and they pride themselves on their relationships with others. If you want to be successful when it comes to relationships, you've got an advantage because of your empathic, caring and sincere nature. You need to ensure that your needs are met and are reciprocated. Don't be afraid to re-evaluate the relationships in your life and be aware of how you feel and act in response to others. *Does it bring out the best or the worse in you?* Work on being your best *self* and don't rely on others to shape this judgement. Once you've worked on yourself and know who you are, you can start to build positive relationships that are personal and professional, so you can ensure you handle them appropriately. Again, being aware of yourself, your traits and your triggers can help you to assess the healthy path so you can ensure you don't stray into unhealthy levels.

Success is at your feet, so don't let your fear of being unworthy, your want of being needy and your desire to feel loved, hold you back. Work on yourself and set some goals – *what does success mean to you? What do you really want in life?* One of the keys to success is to stop looking for validation. This should be first thing you aim to change. As feelings are important to you, start your day off by exercising. Exercising makes us feel good about ourselves and happy. It can really boost our motivation for the day too!

Using the enneagram to achieve self-improvement

It's fantastic if you're looking at ways to self-improvement. There's always room for improvement in everything we do. Having a clingy and needy side is nothing to be ashamed of but it something we can improve.

The Helper doesn't always realise what a selfless and supportive person they are – if this is you, then stop right now! You must appreciate and nurture yourself and your very being.

If you're *The Helper* and you want to improve yourself,

you need to:

- Set boundaries, especially personal boundaries and ensure you take care of yourself. Take plenty of rest and work on yourself.
- Develop a level of acceptance – you can't please everyone (even though you would like to).
- Be conscious and aware of your clingy and needy behaviors, emotions and thoughts. Recognise how this affects yourself and others.
- You must learn to value yourself and develop your knowledge of your own self-worth.
- Question your own motives and don't be afraid to ask why – *why did you decide to do *this* or help *him*?* And don't look for praise when you do. You don't need it!

If you want to get better at something, the first step is to think about what you really want in life and spend some time reflecting and figuring out how you're going to get there. Again, goal setting is great!

Strengthening Relationships – tapping into your own strengths

The Helper is all about the relationships they have with people, because they care and they tend to give, give, give. There's nothing more they like than others needing them, but we need to maintain that at a healthy level.

The Helper is sincere, which makes them a great person to have a relationship with because they are honest and trustworthy. Their caring nature means that they look out and take care of others, because they just can't help it. *The Helper* should ensure that they don't become too possessive and needy in a relationship, because this can lead to the relationship becoming unhealthy too.

Here are 7 top tips to stop being needy in a relationship:

1. Be independent and live your own life. It's important that you have your own hobbies and are independent. It's nice to care and rely on others, but we also need to be self-sufficient. It gives us confidence, and it gives others

confidence in us too!

2. Don't be overbearing. There are people out there who love you – your friends, family, and partners for instance. When someone is overbearing it becomes suffocating.

3. Let go of the past. It's no good holding onto things we can't control and change. Dwelling on the past is extremely unhealthy and it can have such a negative impact on us. Try to think of any past events or experiences as a learning curve. Then you can learn from this and move on.

4. Don't try to change the other person. Remember that you built a relationship with a person because you love them for who they are. Human beings, especially in close relationships (life partners or spouses, and children), we all grow together. That means we change, but it's because we evolve. Development of a relationship needs to be positive – you should trust someone more, feel comfortable, and help each other flourish, together. There's no space for negativity as it can be damaging.

5. Always look for the cause of a problem at its

root. Sometimes what we believe is the problem, isn't. We have to dig a little deeper by asking ourselves why. If we feel sad or angry, we have to ask why we feel like that. If we feel someone else is to blame, it's down to us to find out why we think it's that person – you should focus on your own feelings and actions, rather what you think someone else 'made' you do or feel. It's then down to us to find a solution – to not feel sad or angry as a result of the actions of others. Too many times we try to blame others for how we feel or act, when we should be questioning why we let things bother us, or why we feel or act in a particular way. Only then can you solve the problem at the root of its cause. As we mentioned earlier, we shouldn't try to change others, but we can control our reaction to different behaviors.

6. Be thankful for what you've got and control your jealousy – don't let it be a problem. Think of all the things you have that you are thankful for… See, sometimes we lose sight of what we've got and focus on the things we don't. It's an

unnecessary way to behave because it just makes us think and feel in a negative way. Count your blessings daily and don't let the green-eyed monster out. A wise person said that some level of jealousy is helpful – it keeps us motivated. It's known that *The Helper* is very driven, so be thankful for what you've got, acknowledge any jealousy, and use it to drive you towards achieving your goals. Don't let jealousy consume you, it's a relationship extinguisher and it will soon put out the flame. Use it to appreciate your relationships and improve them – keep your jealousy at a healthy level. If you start to feel in an irrational way, take yourself away and reflect. Awareness is the first step, so don't be afraid to take positive action.

7. Trust others and be open about any issues you have. It's important to put your trust in others in the same way that you expect others to trust you. When you are *The Helper,* you care for people but first, they have to trust you This trust needs to be mutual because all healthy relationships are equal and affection is

reciprocated. One way to show you trust one another is to be open. If you struggle with confidence, feel needy or jealous, tell the other person that you're currently working on this before it becomes an issue. They may be able to shed some insight and if your relationship is equal, they will support and help you, just like you would if you were them.

The Helper certainly wants to feel love and affection when it comes to their relationship and that's fine. They just need to make sure that they aren't overbearing, and that the relationship is mutual. *The Helper* is sincere and should expect this in return. They are sometimes people-pleasers, but they need to be strong and ensure they lead their own life. This is much more desirable when you're in a relationship. You have a voice and you must show this in everything you do.

The Helper is very caring and interpersonal, so they are great communicators and easy to talk to. They are well natured, but they do need to work on their self-development to help them grow. Remember that relationships are not just for show, so check your motives, be as independent as possible and learn to control your possessiveness. Make sure relationships are equal and not one-sided, and constantly assess them. *What are your motives? (Relationship Type 2 with Type 2 — The Enneagram Institute, 2020)*[xx].

Achieving your career potential

The Helper has some great career prospects. They would be really good in a role that involves people, and a job that requires you to care. This could be a job caring for people; maybe a nurse, a lawyer, a teacher, a customer service role, or someone who works in a community, charitable, or social setting. There's no doubt that *The Helper* will go out of their way to help others and they will be good at what they do, because they're so passionate about it. Being completely client or customer focused is a great strength that you can use to progress your career.

If you care for your colleagues too, you will make an inspirational leader. *The Helper* is said to be driven, and leaders inspire and motivate others. They are also good listeners and generous with their time.

To progress in your career, ensure you work on your ability to set boundaries, set clear goals of focus and learn how to say no. Keep your motives in check, and don't seek out recognition, although, if you are a leader you should give lots of recognition to your team. Ensure you take time to build your confidence and keep your needy emotions in check for you, as this is the key to your success.

We all have a dream career and you should certainly aim for yours:

- Create some career goals that are focused solely around what you want. Make sure you break them down into smaller goals or objectives, so that you can create your own steps – then you'll know exactly how you can achieve your goals.
- Consider your personality based on the Enneagram. *How can your strengths help you?*

How can you overcome your weaknesses?
- Think about the skills you need to develop to enable you to achieve your dream career. These can be for your personal development, qualifications and training or experience you might.
- Don't shy away from learning. Be a good student, as you are a teacher. Ensure that constructive criticism isn't seen as a personal attack, but a way to grow. Think about how you can use it to develop and grow.

For *The Helper,* there is an important focus on self-development to help them grow in confidence and independence. Maybe some assertiveness training would be useful too. With your dynamic nature, you have a lot to give so believe! (Enneagram Type 2 - The Caregiver, 2020)[xxi].

Master your finances by honing your skills

The Helper likes to help others and often this can come at their own expense as they sacrifice their time or money. They need to be careful with their money and set some clear boundaries. As they like to be needed and depended upon, they are prone to being generous, but their generosity can be reckless.

If you want to master your finances, all is not lost and there are some things you can do:

- Use a book or spreadsheet and figure out all of your finances. Note down your incomings, any expenditures, and financial commitments. Make sure everything is there, on one sheet including any savings or debts.
- Detail some clear financial goals for yourself. Maybe you want to get out of debt or save for a new house or car... Be specific!
- Create your own money mantra – ask yourself *can I afford it? Do I want it? Do I need it?* If the answer is no to any of these questions, then you should really be considering whether or not you spend your money.
- Be strong – give yourself an allowance and don't be sucked into helping others financially,

constantly. Of course, we love to help family and friends, but just be careful that you're not taken advantage of due to your caring nature. Don't let your neediness cloud your judgements.

When managing your finances your generosity can certainly be your downfall, but your sincerity can strengthen your ability to manage your money. Being aware of your financial situation and your financial goals is certainly a great place to start. When it comes to finances, being honest with yourself about your situation is really important. As you work on your personal development and build-up your assertiveness and confidence, you will get better at handling your money.

We can all make savings when it comes to our money, so if you don't know where to start, go and see a financial advisor. If you have some savings, consider investing your savings but again, take professional advice and work out what methods are best for you.

The Helper is a great listener, so they are susceptible

to taking advice from professionals in the bank or a financial advisor. Make sure you feel in control. Because you constantly feel the need to spend on others and lack confidence, you should make sure you celebrate your wins, just to show recognition that you're heading in the right direction.

It's time to take back control of your finances!

Build emotional, mental, and physical health practices that work best for *The Helper*

Emotional, mental and physical health practices are important for *The Helper* but learning them isn't always simple. That's because of your nature!

As you can be caring and needy, you need to ensure that you maintain healthy, or at least average levels when it comes to the Enneagram. Remember that you should seek advice from a qualified medical professional if you suffer from emotional, mental and physical health issues.

For you, awareness is the first step to improve your health. You need to be aware of any behaviors that can become erratic. The best thing to do is keep a journal that details your behaviors. You should note down times when your motives deviate (when you want to help others so that you feel better or because you need to feel valued or wanted), any time you become too needy, or when your self-confidence dips or you feel worthless (or at least fear being worthless and it gets excessive).

Your emotions are connected to your mental health, because as *The Helper,* you feel passionate about helping and supporting others, and the need for this is connected to your feelings and emotions. They aren't so easily controlled, but we do need to keep them in check. Once you recognise your behaviors and emotions, you can work to change them. Talk to others about any issues you have and if you feel like you would benefit from some training (assertiveness or self-esteem) or counselling, take it. Personal support can really encourage us to open-up which can prove our mental and emotional well-being.

Remember, *The Helper,* can become overbearing, patronizing and manipulating. They can feel compelled to become a martyr, which can mean they become domineering and lose their sense of rationale. This is the type of behaviors that you should be looking out for because they are not healthy.

Don't focus and stress on what others think or do, and shift your focus to yourself, what you want, and what you need to do, for you! If you find yourself resorting to negative behaviors ask yourself, *what triggered this? Why do I feel this way?* Once you're aware, you still need to probe further to find the trigger or cause. Never underestimate the importance of your own emotional wellbeing.

To promote your physical, mental and emotional wellbeing for *The Helper,* there are some personality:

- Swimming – Swimming is a great way to exercise as it uses every part of the body. It's a cardio exercise and 20 minutes each day can make you feel good about yourself.

- Meditation – Meditation can really help you to relax and collect your thoughts. As you can be irrational or feel needy at times, this is a great way to collect your thoughts and maintain a healthy mind.
- Hiking – Taking a longer walk or hike can be really invigorating. Again, it gives you time to collect your thoughts and sometimes we can sort through our thoughts, feelings and emotions. It can also be great when working through any problems or issues too.

Become a Leadership Rockstar with your Enneagram skillset

At their best, *The Helper* can make a great leader because of their caring nature. They are good at praising others and they are very compassionate. *The Helper* is very encouraging and driven, which means that they can motivate others easily. They love being involved in the lives of others and take an interest because they want to help them. They can always see the strengths in others and can provide others their undivided attention. Nothing is ever too much for the helper, and they love to promote others and innovation. They are very humble and unselfish, which means they are great at pushing others and giving credit where credit is due.

In order to transform their skills as a leader, *The Helper* must embrace their assertive side. While it's fine to instil confidence in your team and rely on them, ensure you aren't too needy. They need to increase their self-confidence and ensure a fair environment because *The Helper* always wants to do what's right. Ensure you stick to those principles.

Top Tips to Boost your efficiency through problem-solving methods that work for you

For *The Helper,* problem solving isn't always easy. You need to be able to work well with others. If you're problem-solving at work, talk to your team. If you're problem-solving on a personal level, then you should talk to your own support network – family or friends. The most important thing is to remember that this isn't your problem alone. As a person who is driven, you can work well with others to find the answers!

Think through your problem and write it down. A problem solver needs to be creative. Problem solving needs an innovative approach and this can be based on intuition or it can be a more structured approach. *The Helper* is often great at problem solving already because they are good at managing risks, providing they are in control of their emotions. *The Helper* is not necessarily a risk-taker, so they are capable of weighing up the pros and cons. Problem solvers should have strong rigorous researching skills and they should be logical – brainstorm solutions if a solution isn't obvious. *What are your options? The Helper* can increase their problem-solving skills if they improve their confidence because they need to make informed decision, based on their findings.

Your personality suggests that you will listen to what others think. For *The Helper,* it's important that they are not influenced too much by others and are still able to take advice objectively, but not feel obliged to take it.

Discover a path to spirituality that works best for your personality type

For *The Helper,* a spiritual approach will be very beneficial as there are ways we can practice a positive and healthy approach through spirituality.

First of all, you should practice gratitude. Everyday, think about the things you are thankful and grateful for. Write it down! Many people have a gratitude journal so that every day they are reminded of what they are thankful for. They can also reflect on this when they need to.

If you have a gratitude journal, be careful not to turn it into something that's over the top and focuses on how thankful you are for others. Reflect on things you are grateful for on a personal level and your own personal development too.

Another way to develop spirituality is through yoga, or meditation as mentioned earlier. Try some light yoga and focus on your breathing or try some forms of guided meditation that focus on your inner self, and program the mind. The more you practice spirituality techniques, the more you will grow.

Connect the dots to create a vision for progress and growth

If you think your dominant personality is *The Helper,* it's time to create your vision for personal growth. Let's explore this personality type further.

With every personality type, there are 9 levels of development for each personality type. We should be aiming for healthy levels 1-3, as this is *The Helper* at their best. Levels 4-6 are average levels and they are acceptable, but *The Helper* should be conscious if they start to creep towards level 6. Levels 7-9 are unhealthy levels and if you find yourself at these levels changes need to be made ASAP. *The Helper* can make many positive changes and the way they care for others, should extend to themselves. Believe in yourself!

Check out the levels below and set clear goals. Assess

where you are now and where you want to be, moving forward.

Healthy levels

Level 1 – This level is the best for *The Helper*. They feel privileged to be involved in the lives of others, and are happy to love others, unconditionally, even if there's nothing in it for them. They are not self-centred and show a high level of affection and care for others. They are very humble, compassionate and honest in an empathetic way.

Level 2 – At level 2, *The Helper* is very thoughtful and concerned about others. They care about what others want and wear their heart on their sleeve. They show empathy and are also very forgiving, even when others let them down.

Level 3 – At level 3, *The Helper* shows appreciation for others and they always like to see the good in everyone. They have a nurturing nature and care about others and of themselves too. They are generous, loving and encouraging.

Average levels

Level 4 – At level 4, *The Helper* can become overly friendly. They give a lot of attention to others because they long for close relationships. They are full of good intentions on an emotional level. They believe that love is really important and they remind everyone of that on a regular basis. They often give compliments to others too, to encourage them and begin people-pleasing.

Level 5 – *The Helper* must feel needed at this level and believe that love is everything. They can feel dependant on others but feel that others depend on them. They struggle because they can't do enough for others, yet this wears them out and sometimes they are doing this to make themselves feel better. They sometimes become intimate with others and start to meddle, because they long to control others.

Level 6 – When at level 6, *The Helper* wants to feel self-gratification. They need to be important to others and feel indestructible, so they exaggerate their efforts. They can be over-the-top, patronizing and they often presume too much. They long to be the hero!

Unhealthy levels

Level 7 – *The Helper* becomes very self-serving when at level 7. They resort to manipulation and don't think twice about putting others on guilt trips. Sometimes, they self-sabotage themselves to get sympathy from others. By this time, they often start to belittle others and can become very selfish and aggressive. They start to deceive others and like to remind others how much they 'owe' them.

Level 8 – At this level, *The Helper* starts to feel entitled and becomes extremely manipulative. They sabotage others and become a dominant force. They start to make demands of others and at times are known to insist on receiving money or repayments of debts. They have also been known to coerce sexual favors too. They believe they have the right to get anything they want at any cost.

Level 9 – This is the lowest level and at level 9, *The Helper* uses excuses regarding their behavior. They fall apart and can start to suffer with health problems and can develop a personality, but sometimes this is fictitious. They become bitter and resentful, and often point the finger of being abused. They rationalize their own behavior by insisting they are the victim. They use all of this and become a burden on others, because the need they have for others to be in their life.

Anyone who hits the unhealthy levels, must seek professional medical advice right away. Well done for recognizing the signs – you've made the first step, but you must go visit your doctor! If you are average or healthy, you can start to plan your path of improvement and personal growth path. Again, you can do this by setting goals. Even if you're at level 1, you need a maintenance plan, so you're not off the hook yet. We can all make improvements or maintain/develop aspects of ourselves – keep going! (The Enneagram Institute, 2020)[xxii]

Affirmations for *The Helper*

I value my goals and boundaries.
I am strong, independent and I believe in myself.
I love and respect others for who they are. I love and respect myself for who I am.

Chapter 4

Type Three: The Achiever

Do you live for success? Do you crave achievements and are you motivated to get what you want in life? The next Enneagram personality type is certainly driven by success. This is type three: *The Achiever.* They are self-assured and alluring. Their confidence shines through and this is infectious. People admire *The Achiever* and they are drawn to them! If people are drawn to your confidence, this could be you!

Introduction to *The Achiever:*

The Achiever is very ambitious. They need to excel in life and their energy can fill the room. They are confident, charming and attractive in both looks and nature. They control themselves well, in a calm and professional way but they are concerned with what others think and their own image too.

The Achiever can become a little too competitive. Their biggest problem is their addiction to work – that's right, they are work-a-holics.

PROFILE: *The Achiever*

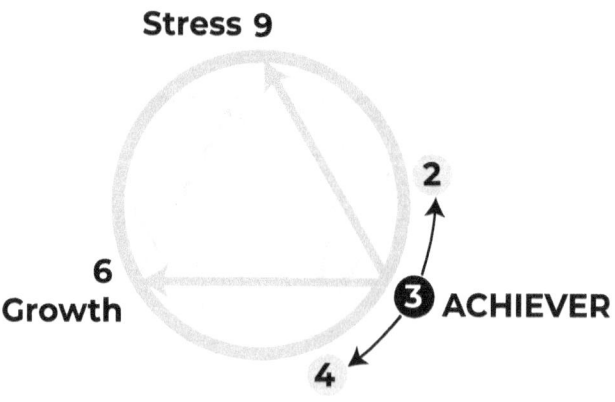

Key Desire: They need to be valuable and feel a sense of self-worth.

Key Fear: They fear being unwanted and worthless.

Wings possibilities: If you hate feeling and are ambitious, it's likely that you're Enneagram type three with a two-wing, you're the *Charmer*. If you are controlled and restrained in nature you could have a four-wing, and that would make you *The Professional*.

Three with a two-wing: If you have a two-wing, you are *The Charmer* and you show traits from type two, as well as your dominant personality being a type three. You want to be valued, but only by your accomplishments. You are great at setting goals and staying focused, but sometimes you can focus too much on your social appearance. (Enneagram Type 3w2 – The Enchanter, 2020)[xxiii].

Three with a four-wing: If you are type three, with a four-wing, then you are *The Professional*. The professional is attentive, practical and efficient. They always look to improve but sometimes they focus too heavily on success and find it difficult to accept disappointments in life (Enneagram Type 3w4 - The

Expert, 2020)[xxiv].

Key motivations: *The Achiever* wants to stand out from the crowd and draw attention to themselves. They love the admiration they get from others and they strive to impress.

Strengths: *The Achiever* is driven, adaptable, and they often excel in everything they do.

Stress points and Growth: They can become deceitful and vain. If they follow the arrow of integration (growth) to number 6, they often become more committed and they are often more cooperative too. When following the direction of disintegration (stress) towards number 9, they can feel disengaged. For *The Achiever,* over-stressing the body can happen through exhaustion as they think they have to do things themselves. It's important to maintain your energy levels but be careful that you don't rely on stimulants such as coffee as this can make you worse (The Enneagram Institute, 2020)[xxv].

How *The Achiever* can hack their own success?

The Achiever has the ability to become great, but they have to work out what that means. They can hack their own success easily, because success is what they live for. They are accomplished, gracious and happy, and they have a magnetic personality. They are a figure of authority and authenticity. They are well liked and popular amongst their friends, family and peers. Their contributions to society make them role models as they are headstrong, with constant developing talents.

The Achiever, can hack their own success by using their influence to get what they want. They must be careful not to make this their key focus and it's important for them to maintain a healthy balance between work, personal and family, and self-care. If the balance isn't right, and everything is materialistic, the achiever will never be happy. A nice car, money, and the biggest house you can afford does not instil happiness. *The Achiever* wants to be valued and they live to inspire. They love culture but they need to spend time enjoying it, rather than admiring it from the office window.

The Achiever has some work to do on themselves. They already have the tools they need to be successful, but they need to make sure they get the balance before they hit burn-out. In order to hack a healthy level of success, *The Achiever* need to go on a journey of self-development.

The main thing to work out is what you want and for that, you will have to dig deep. Life is more than a show and although encouragement and admiration are nice, its important to affirm that for ourselves, rather than from what others say. One person's success is not the same as another, so take a notepad right now and write down what success is to you, why you need it, and when you want it. *What happens if you don't get it?*

When success comes so naturally to you, it's difficult to say how to hack it. There are some simple tips to help you succeed:

- Ensure you're the right person for the task – *what skills do you need and when can you achieve them? What experience and personal qualities do you need? What makes you the right person?*

- Surround yourself with the right people, preferably those who are successful. If you want success in a particular field, putting yourself in the right place with the right people matters.
- Aim high, sell your dreams and know your market. If we want to inspire, we need to be reaching for the stars. Push for something bigger and be excited about what you want and what the future holds. Ensure you know your market and what trends are hot now. Knowing the latest fashion, products, news and market trends could be key to your success. There's nothing worse than someone who doesn't know what they're talking about.

Success of this level is fine – you got this! The biggest thing that *The Achiever* can learn if they want to be truly successful is the importance of themselves. Their health, values, wants and needs all matter. Success isn't everything so make sure you're meeting your basic needs too, or your relationships and health could suffer.

Using the enneagram to achieve self-improvement

When you are successful, it can be difficult to find ways to self-improve. As *The Achiever,* you have a great ethos and personality. You have a charming nature, a high-status level, and you're climbing the tree of advancement. That doesn't mean there isn't room for improvement, *does it?*

The Achiever often becomes over-competitive and they have an addictive personality – they are addicted to work. This can cause numerous health problems both mentally and physically, so it's important to focus on your own wellbeing and maintain a healthy balance. Your need to impress others can also become unhealthy and encourage you to deceive others. It's also important that your vanity doesn't get the better of you – you don't need recognition to affirm your achievements!

If you're *The Achiever* and you want to improve yourself, you should focus on yourself. You can do this by:

- Write yourself some personal, work and well-being goals. This will help you to explore what you really want to achieve next.
- Set some boundaries and stick to them. If you work too much, set clear boundaries that you can stick to. They should help you to create a suitable plan and allow you to take time for rest and for yourself.
- Be aware of any issues that hold you back. Your obsessiveness with work, your competitiveness, your vanity, and ensure you work on them. While high achievers with personality are attractive features, overconfidence and vanity can repel others.
- Write a plan of action and use your calendar to plot out your day – why not try time-blocking and ensure you spend quality time each week with family, friends and working on yourself (or some related activities).
- Consider ways to maintain your mental and physical health effectively. *What activities can you do that will improve your physical health? What can you do to ensure your mental health develops and improves too?*

The Achiever has a vision, so what's yours? Make sure you spend some time reflecting on the important things in life, before you go any further.

Strengthening Relationships – tapping into your own strengths

The Achiever is friendly and social, so they are great in relationships. They are optimistic and can encourage their friends, partners and family members in everything they do. They want to be loved, as most people do, but they can also be sensitive too. As they are success-orientated, this can take over and they need to feel valued, but sometimes neglect to value others. This isn't intentional and they are approachable and adaptable.

The Achiever is honest, and people appreciate this in a relationship. Their charismatic personality makes them attractive in a relationship but sometimes they can be harsh on others and be overly critical when offering their views. This can come across as a personal attack and something you should avoid. Make sure you take time to enjoy and nurture your relationships as love and affection needs to be reciprocated, whether this be a personal, work, sexual or paternal/maternal relationship.

If you are work orientated and struggle in your relationships due to the pressures, here are a few tips on how you can maintain positive relationships:

1. Spend quality time together. It's not always about the quantity of time but the quality. Ensure the other person has your undivided attention. It's better than spending a larger amount of time and being distracted or on your cell phone.
2. Recognize the other person and find out what's happening in their life. Share intimate details and find out how the other person is doing, what's new and anything else you need to know. Show appreciation of time together.
3. Reframe your relationship and talk openly about stresses and problems. Others appreciate honest communication and it gives others the opportunity to open-up too.

4. Always show the other person how you feel. Share a compliment, show affection with a kiss or a hug, a small token gift or words. A simple, *I miss you* or *I love you* goes a long way!
5. Talk about your hopes and dreams and make plans for the future. Think about what's next for you or anything you can do together. For example, if it's your best friend, arrange to go out and have dinner next time, so you have more time. Take an actionable step to ensure it happens.

The Achiever is great at maintaining most positive relationships, but sometimes personal relationships suffer if work is a priority. They are good at calming others and their irresistible personality allows them to rectify any issues in a relationship. Remember, be honest, but kind. Don't be harsh as it can come across as aggressive. You are a people person and you're in tune with what others want, so this is often easy for *The Achiever,* providing they are willing to step away from their work and dedicate time to relationship building.

When it comes to relationships, you have needs and expectations, so you must make sure that you meet the needs and expectations of the people you have relationships too. A relationship cannot be one-sided, so both parties must contribute and participate (Relationship Type 3 with Type 3 — The Enneagram Institute, 2020)[xxvi].

Achieving your career potential

The career options are vast and wide for *The Achiever*. Chances are, they are already on the path to where they want to be if they are not there already. They are great when it comes to business and strategy. They have a lot of experience, skills and are possibly even highly educated (not necessarily with qualifications, but nonetheless, they are educated).

The Achiever would work well in management or business roles, or in careers such as medicine or science, in something that they can excel. *The Achiever* may even be an entrepreneur or business owner. They have no issues with job interviews because they are confident and professional. They have a personality that attracts others, and they are motivated to get what they want in life.

As they are success-orientated, they often excel in their role. They are motivated and pragmatic in their approach, and their adaptability allows them to immerse themselves into any situation.

The Achiever makes a great leader. They like to distinguish themselves from everyone else as they like to impress. You don't need attention or affirmation from others, because you are already worthy and competent. Diplomacy is also a great skill that *The Achiever* is known to have. Their energy is infectious, and they are poised and professional. They are committed and can be very cooperative which means they are great people to work with or employees to hire.

To progress in your career, you need to ensure that your self-assurance does not grow into vanity. As *The Achiever* fears being worthless, they can feel pressurized into being deceitful. Once they begin deceiving, the harder it is to come back from and people stop trusting you. Ensure you don't allow yourself to stray into that territory as it can be damaging for your career.

Even if success is at your fingertips, you should still have plans for your future career. Think about what your dream career is and aim for this:

- Find out what you really want and write down for yourself some career goals.
- Ensure you have boundaries that separate your work/career from your personal life.
- Consider any skills, experience, training, or qualifications that you may need to look into before you can progress your career. *Is this possible? How soon? When do you see yourself in your dream job?*
- Consider your personality based on the Enneagram and compare it to your chosen career and career goals. *How can your strengths help you? How can you overcome your weaknesses?*

- Record and monitor your progress as you strive towards your career. As you like recognition for your achievements, this is a great way to develop and maintain your motivation.

The main thing for *The Achiever* is to focus on yourself, personally, so you can strive for your career and get that work-life balance that you need. There's no doubt that *The Achiever* will get what they want when it comes to their career, because they are driven and unstoppable (Enneagram Type 3 - The Performer, 2020)[xxvii].

Master your finances by honing your skills

The Achiever is usually great with their finances. They know what success is and they are highly organised which means they are sensible when it comes to matters of money. However, there are occasions when *The Achiever* spends money in a reckless way and often this is to do with self-image. They want the best of everything!

If you want to master your finances, there are some

things that you can do to ensure you only spend what you can afford:

- Ensure you set your budget and stick to it. If you're thinking about splashing your cash on those designer shoes or that new hair style and color, just think twice and ask yourself; *have I set a budget for that this month?* We agree, image is important, but it's important for you to monitor your spends.
- Create a record of your incomings and outgoings. We need to be aware and in control of our own finances. This way, you will know your status every month.
- Stop buying on impulse. Make sure you plan your finances for the month in advance and be strict – if you haven't planned for it, put it in for next month and save for what you want. The stricter we are, the more we'll appreciate it and it shows discipline too.
- Write some financial goals – what do you want and what should save for in your future? Don't be afraid to seek advice and invest your savings

in a way that suits you. If you have any debts, make sure you write a plan to deal with this and think about how quickly you can get this done.

Financial stability is important so it's important to curb impulsive spending. Use your skills as an organized and realistic person to manage your finances. That's not to say you can't spend anything, just think twice about those pricey spends.

Assess your spending status and seek out professional advice from your bank or a financial advisor if you need to make savings or have money to invest. They can give you valuable advice on how to handle your money in a more effective way.

You're often tempted to spend money on your image, but you look great already. You're all about the value, so value your finances and take back the control. You got this!

Build emotional, mental, and physical health practices that work best for *The Achiever*

The Achiever is at risk of damaging their physical and mental health as a result of their nature to work and achieve. This can mean constant pressure is placed on you, which can lead to stress, increased competitiveness and the obsession with work or careers. It's time to look after yourself and your personal needs.

You can learn to fulfill your emotional, mental and physical health and figure out what works best for you. If you find yourself stuck at work in a stressful environment or in front of a screen all day, you will need a break to rest. Take yourself off for a brisk walk – it's not only good for your health, but it can invigorate the mind and give you the break you need.

Remember that you should seek advice from a qualified medical professional if you suffer from emotional, mental and physical health issues. This could be stress or anxiety formed through work, due to the pressures you put on yourself. Don't be afraid to get help if you need it. This isn't always as simple as it sounds for *The Achiever,* because they are so focused on getting what they want.

The first step to improve your mental and physical health is showing awareness of any issues you may have. This means recognizing any negative or destructive thoughts, feelings or behaviors that you may have. Watch out for when you feel pressured, worthless, or extra-competitive. Seek help immediately if you realize you're being deceitful too – you're only deceiving yourself in the long-term. This indicates you need a break and you need to take a step back and reflect.

Time blocking is a great way for you to get the balance you need between your work, education and personal life. Print out your calendar and schedule in time with your family and friends. Schedule in work, and time for exercise and personal time/care too. Time for you is important for personal growth purposes, which often makes us more productive in the things we do.

You need to have a certain level of self-awareness, so set boundaries when it comes to your health, and ensure you're scheduling in everything you need. Caring for yourself and saying no, isn't weak. You are showing strength if you stick to your boundaries.

To promote your physical, mental and emotional wellbeing for *The Achiever,* there are some things you can do:

- Take a brisk walk – walking fast can soothe the mind. It's good exercise, provides us with fresh air, and it can be invigorating.
- Swimming – swimming can be relaxing, and it doesn't take a lot of time. Fit in a few laps in the morning before you go to work.
- Pilates – Pilates is a great form of exercise that works your core and promotes good mental and physical health and wellbeing. 30 minutes of Pilates can really help you focus.

Become a Leadership Rockstar with your Enneagram skillset

At their best, *The Achiever* can make a great leader

because they are built for success. They have an undeniable persistence that drives them forward and they are able to motivate others too. *The Achiever* often has a strong personal philosophy so that they can reason well with problems and with others. Their performance is increased, and they have high expectations of themselves and others, along with strong principles.

The Achiever is well driven but in order to be an effective leader, they need to ensure that they don't cause themselves to become exhausted as they aren't at their best when this happens. They should also develop their social awareness by working as a team towards goals and ensuring that they include everyone. They are great at finding their own value and progressing their career, but they have the potential to motivate others into becoming high achievers too.

The Achiever shouldn't be afraid to take breaks as this makes them into a better leader. Their ambition is something that others find attractive and they desire to be accepted amongst others. Try not to dwell on this, instead focus on your personal, team or career goals. Focusing on specific goals give us better insight.

Being truthful is a key personality trait that will take them far in their role as a leader, but they need to be able to express their honesty in a professional and constructive way, as sometimes this can be confused with anger. Tiring out yourself and the team can lead to burn out, so encourage your team to take care of themselves. It's also important that you lead by example – leaders lead the way.

In order to transform their skills as a leader, embrace your ambitious side, and train others to have a similar mindset (at healthy levels of course). Always aim for value, and ensure your team understand your expectations and standards. In fact, it's a good idea to create a set of core values and invest time in helping your team devise their own while working in a way that's beneficial for the business. Ensure that you don't lose sight of your feelings and your own personal needs as this is for the greater good.

The Achiever aims to be the best, always, so when they are a leader, there is no difference in their attitude and drive. The difference is, they have more responsibility which means they must set examples, because others will look to them for inspiration and guidance. You are meant to be a leader, so maintain the healthy levels and thrive. This is what you were born to do!

Top Tips to Boost your efficiency through problem-solving methods that work for you

The Achiever has already proved themselves time and time again when it comes to problem solving methods. They are quick and innovative thinkers, they are methodical, logical and strategic, and their confidence means that they are strong.

There are some tips that can be shared to improve efficiency, but *The Achiever,* may know or use some of these techniques already. Especially if they've problem-solved in the past:

- Clearly identify the problem – *what is the*

problem? What caused the problem? Why is it a problem? It's best if you write this down.
- Research the problem. Don't be afraid to search online – *How can I solve [problem]?*
- When problem solving, *The Achiever* should not try to do this alone and should involve others. Complete a brainstorming session with others if possible, or if not, ask for the opinion of others who are familiar with the problem or know you.
- Always carefully assess your options, and ensure you weigh up the positives and negatives. Always ask yourself why when it comes to your solution. Don't just choose the solution you prefer, choose the one that is best or most effective. *Why are you choosing that particular solution?*
- You're already a strong person, so use your assertiveness, intelligence and drive to solve problems effectively, innovatively, and efficiency.

Your personality suggests that your problem-solving techniques are great, but you can soon extend them, so that they are outstanding. Consult with others, do your research, and use strategies and creativity when responding to your problem. If you have a good team or support network, you can become formidable when solving problems. Don't forget to thank and recognize those that help you arrive at an informed decision.

Discover a path to spirituality that works best for your personality type

The Achiever is driven by success and achievement, so they are not necessarily spiritual. That's a shame, because they would really benefit by being in touch with their spiritual side.

As you have such a busy life, it's important to concentrate on acts with the mind. For you, it's best to adjust your thinking patterns because you genuinely want to become a better person.

If you want to be a better person then you need to train your brain to think more positively. The best things to do are:

- Walk away from negative situations. Watching and hearing negative behavior is draining.
- Don't participate with your own inner dialogues if they start to be negative. There's nothing to gain.
- Work on changing your negative thoughts and don't allow them to affect your state of mind. They can cloud your judgement. Steer clear of them and change them into something positive. Every time you feel negative, spin this around and use it as a learning curve. *What have you learned? What would you do different? How can you improve?*
- Don't allow events that are difficult or disappointing to affect your logical thinking or moods. Use your problem-solving techniques to overcome these obstacles.

When you can manage your thoughts and change your thinking patterns or outlook, you can start to reflect on your life. Taking time to relax and reflect on how you can become a better person can really help.

If you feel that you are not really a spiritual person, why not try a holistic therapy, like Color Therapy. This would be ideal for you as it is said that the energy we receive from color and lights can improve our emotional, mental and physical wellbeing. Colors are known to have different effects on us, and this is a very non-invasive, holistic therapy. You can have a therapist who specialises in Color Therapy provide you with a session and they will use lighting and colors during your therapy. This is thought to lift your mood, and each color is said to have healing powers. It can sometimes be used along with other therapies, such as aromatherapy or Indian head massage. This is a relaxing therapy that can help you think clearly. If you're a busy person, this is certainly worth a try, but note, that this should be done regularly.

Connect the dots to create a vision for progress and growth

If you think your dominant personality type is *The Achiever,* then you probably already have a clear vision for your personal growth and progress. The question is, *have you committed this this? Have you written down your plans and detailed your future goals?*

Let's look at the 9 levels of development for this personality type. We should be aiming for healthy levels 1-3, as this is *The Achiever* at their best. Levels 4-6 are average levels and they are acceptable but as *The Achiever,* you may not see it that way as you always want to be the best. Levels 7-9 are unhealthy levels and if you find yourself these levels you need to think about the changes you can make. *The Achiever* can make many positive changes to their life and it can help them develop and grow. They are hungry to learn which makes them the ideal candidates to strive for their healthy levels and succeed. Remember to set yourself clear goals and assess what you need to do to move forward.

Healthy levels
Level 1 – This level is the best for *The Achiever.* They are very modest and charitable, with great humor. Everything that they do is from their heart. They are authentic, self-directed, and very gentle. They accept

others and themselves, and they are everything they appear to be and want to be.

Level 2 – At level 2, *The Achiever* has high energy levels and oozes self-esteem. They are more than competent in everything they do, and they believe in themselves. They are both gracious and charming, yet they adapt well to change and challenges. Time after time, they prove themselves valuable.

Level 3 – At level 3, *The Achiever* remains ambitions, and they want to be the very best they can be. They strive for their ideal and constantly improve themselves. They are motivated, effective, admired, have a wide range of qualities and skills which they often become outstanding in, and they crave to constantly improve.

Average levels
Level 4 – At level 4, *The Achiever* loves to climb the social ladder and is afraid of failing. They need recognition in order to feel worthy. They start to compare themselves with others and look for status and success. They are invested in their future and long to

be the best. They are also high performers and very career focused.

Level 5 – *The Achiever* starts to become image conscious at level 5. They are in danger of losing themselves as they ignore their own needs and feelings. They have high expectations and start to have problems with authenticity and closeness.

Level 6 – When at level 6, *The Achiever* is desperate to impress others. They are self-promoting, superior and are starting to feel jealous against others. They can be seen as exhibitionists, but they show many narcissistic tendencies. They believe in their own talents but show some level of arrogance.

Unhealthy levels
Level 7 – *The Achiever* has strong fears that they allow to control their attitudes and actions. They fear being humiliated and failure, but they are desperate to preserve themselves and their reputation. They can exploit others and use underhanded tactics to get ahead.

Level 8 – At this level, *The Achiever* starts to be overly jealous of others. They start to be malicious and they aren't afraid to sabotage others so that they can get ahead. They try to hide their mistakes to avoid exposure, but this shows that they are untrustworthy.

Level 9 – This is the lowest level and at level 9, *The Achiever* is vindictive and could be displaying signs of Narcissistic Personality Disorder. They are obsessive about their own failures and will do anything to hide them. They don't think twice about ruining the happiness of others, and they demonstrate worrying behavior.

If you are *The Achiever,* you should be cautious as you start to get to levels 6-9. You should certainly seek professional medical advice and deal with any issues in the correct way, that's most effective for you. The best thing you can do is build up an awareness of what level you are at now and what level we want to be. It's a good idea to make yourself familiar with each level so that you can recognize the signs, if your personality drops to unhealthy levels. If you are at average or healthy levels, you need to look to improve or maintain your levels. Write yourself a plan, with goals so you can record and monitor your progress as you follow your growth plan. It will ensure personal success! (The Enneagram Institute, 2020)[xxviii]

Affirmations for *The Achiever*

Teamwork is amazing. Nobody is smarter than many of us.

I am capable, empowered and strong.

I embrace my imperfections every day. I learn to accept and improve.

Chapter 5

Type Four: The Individualist

The Individualist sometimes need help finding themselves. *Do you draw a blank when someone asks you who you are? Maybe, you sometimes try to create an identity, or search for your purpose?* You might be creative, but you might not know where you fit in. This next Enneagram personality type is creative and personal, and they are *The Individualist: Type Four*. They can sometimes be dramatic, but they enjoy expression themselves. Let's find out more about this personality and how we can develop it.

Introduction to *The Individualist*:

The Individualist is often a sensitive soul. They are reserved, and creative, but they tend to hideaway their true selves. This because they don't feel confident in who they are or what they are doing in life and this can leave them quite vulnerable. This lack of identity can lead to mood swings as they can be unhappy with themselves. *The Individualist* has the potential to be an inspiration to others. They are great at transforming themselves and starting fresh, provided they don't allow their feelings of self-pity or self-indulgence to get the better of them.

PROFILE: *The Individualist*

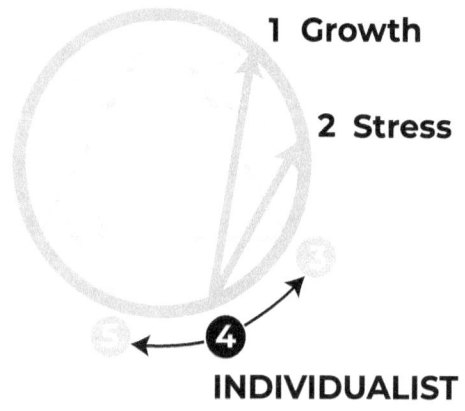

Key Desire: They long to find themselves and their purpose in life.

Key Fear: Lack of identity scares them.

Wings possibilities: If you like to be unique and want to leave your impact on the world, you could be Enneagram type four with a three-wing, and that means you are the *The Aristocrat.* If you are creative and smart, and have a need to understand the world, you could have a five-Wing. This makes you *The Bohemian.*

Four with a three-wing: If you have a three-wing, your are *The Aristocrat.* You are in tune with yourself, and you always strive to be authentic. You are a creative thinker, but sometimes your self-doubt holds you back (Enneagram Type 4w3 - The Enthusiast, 2020)[xxix].

Four with a five-wing: If you have a five-wing, you are *The Bohemian.* They are curious and have a strong need for knowledge. They can solve problems creatively, but sometimes they can withdraw from the people around them, when it would be in their best interests to keep up connections with others (Enneagram Type 4w5 -

The Free Spirit, 2020)[xxx].

Key motivations: *The Individualist* likes elegance and beauty. They try to surround themselves in such things and live to protect their self-image. They love the opportunity to express themselves, but sometimes this is difficult. They long to know themselves and aim for their lifegoals, once they've figured them out.

Strengths: *The Individualist* is sensitive and expressive. Their creativity is a key strength and they have the ability to inspire others.

Stress points and Growth:

As they move into the path of disintegration towards number 2 (stress), a type four can become clingy and get too involved in certain situations. Following the arrow of integration (growth) can set emotions into a whirl. They can become jealous, but as they head towards number 1, they become very healthy as they are principled and objective (The Enneagram Institute, 2020) [xxxi].

How *The Individualist* can hack their own success?

The Individualist has the ability to become an inspirational person. If they want success, they really need to control their mood, and go on a journey to figure out what they want in life and how they can get it. The most powerful thing they can do, is figure out their own identity and pathway. This will help them increase confidence and take control.

The Individualist should set themselves some inspiring goals for the future. They need to know what they want and how they're going to get there, so if they set future goals, they can work back-over and set smaller steps to achieve those goals.

The Individualist needs to get to know themselves, in order to form a clear identity. You can do this by practicing self-awareness, and this means learning about different parts of your personality and personality. You can become aware of your very being and you can be honest with yourself.

Think about the things you like – your favorite color, best friend, how you like your hair, what clothes you like, and what type of exercise you like. You should also know personal things like what you like reading or watching on TV (if you even like these things).

Another way to hack your success is to practice self-care. We need to meet our own needs and sometimes if we have a lot on or become overwhelmed, it's hard to know ourselves. If you take time to meet your basic needs, take time to destress and reflect on yourself; you can start to get to know yourself again, and be clear when it comes to your identity.

Remember, that you are creative and expressive, so don't be afraid to use those skills when moving forward. You're sensitive, but again, you can use this to your advantage as you are in touch with how others feel and can show a great deal of empathy.

The reason you don't feel strongly enough about your own identity and are always searching for your purpose, is because your confidence is low. Take some time to develop your own confidence by:

- List down the things you think you are good at. If you don't know, ask others – friends, colleagues, family, etc... and ask them, *what's my speciality? If you had to come to me for help or advice, what would do you think I could help you with?* Remember this list and consider what strengths you have to support your skills.
- Create your own self-belief affirmations and repeat them every morning. Remind yourself of these things when you feel glum.
- Prepare in advance and problem solve effectively. Life is full of ups and downs, and you need to be prepared for that. If you have things you want to do, but there are barriers in your way, or they take a lot of energy, plan in advance and prepare yourself well. This way, you are more likely to achieve them, so make sure you research your topic and feel mentally prepared. Increase your problem-solving techniques by strategizing and figuring out your problems. Brainstorm your solutions. When we do things

well, our confidence soars!

Success can be tricky when you struggle to know who you are or what you're good at but you will get there! Once you figure out what you want, your confidence will increase, and you will excel. Success is within your reach!

Using the enneagram to achieve self-improvement

If you want to improve yourself, *The Individualist* needs to build their self-awareness. Many people wonder what it means to be self-aware, and basically it means knowing yourself, but in such a way, that you know and understand why you feel, act and think in a particular way. Self-awareness is based on psychological theories, and it means looking for patterns in the way we think about things that happen and ourselves. *The Individualist* is known to suffer with mood swings, so self-awareness can help us understand how we feel, what makes us tick and what makes us uncomfortable. It helps us to form ideas of what we can do to improve our responses.

If you're *The Individualist* and you want to improve yourself, you should focus on yourself. You can do this by:

- Keep a mood journal. Whenever something makes you feel emotions, write it down. If you feel happy – why? If you feel upset, sad, excited – why?
- Escape for a while by reading a book. Maybe a self-help book or some high-quality fiction. This will help you clear your mind and then you can go back to any arising issues and tackle them with a clear head.
- Use exercise to keep a healthy mind and body. Try walking, swimming, or even running. Exercise gives us something to focus on, but it also gives us more energy. It's great for clearing the mind so we can put things into perspective.

The Individualist has a lot to figure out, but the more they know about themselves, the more self-improvements they can make. Feeling good is good for us so don't be afraid to treat yourself from time to time. A trip to the salon, or a new handbag is ideal.

You could also try meditation to introduce more positivity into your life.

Strengthening Relationships – tapping into your own strengths

The Individualist is known for their sensitivity, and they are also known as being romantic too. Relationships vary – we can have friendships, family relationships, sexual relationships, loving relationships or professional relationships, and each of these require a contribution from two parties. A relationship should be equal, so both of you need to contribute when it comes to relationships. For you in particular, you need to make sure you don't neglect the second person in all of your relationships, because *The Individualist* is known to become self-centred at times.

As *The Individualist,* you have lots of positives to bring to a relationship. You are caring and compassionate, you admire others and inspire them too. As a romantic, you empathise well with others. If you feel like you are becoming overly critical or resentful in your relationships, you must stop yourself from reacting as this can be damaging. Especially if you allow the conflict to escalate and start blaming the other person in your relationship. You can do this by building on your self-awareness (as we mentioned in the last section) as this can help you to control and change your emotions, actions and thoughts in a positive way.

The Individualist can be indecisive about what they want in life and who they are. If you lose a relationship, or it breaks down, this can hit you hard. Mood swings are already a part of your personality, but you need to know how to deal with them in the healthiest way for you. Don't be afraid to talk about how you feel, and if you can't talk to people in your ready-formed relationships, talk to someone else, like a counsellor. Things like breathing exercises, mindfulness or meditation, can help us manage, cope and process such things.

For *The Individualist,* the more they learn about themselves, the stronger they are in a relationship. Don't sell yourself short as you have a lot to offer!

(Relationship Type 4 with Type 4 — The Enneagram Institute, 2020)[xxxii].

Achieving your career potential

There are many career opportunities for *The Individualist*. As a creative person, you have a need to express yourself and this is a great attribute that will help you further your career. You might enjoy things like painting, drawing, acting, dancing or writing to show your creativity.

The Individualist would work well in the creative industries and there are so many possibilities. Arts, museums and theatre work could be ideal, but so could media related fields too. With the power of the internet, there are many design jobs out there too, like website design and content writing. You are a free-spirit and would work well as a freelancer or running your own business. Your creativity is a powerful tool that you can use to attract others because you have a unique way of thinking. You are innovative and have some great ideas, but *The Individualist* prefers to work alone. You sometimes find it difficult to work with others, but learning to be more flexible, adaptable and improving your team working skills could help you take your career to the next level.

The Individualist likes to do things their own way because they like to work with freedom. As you can be self-conscious, you need to ensure this doesn't hold you back. Being self-conscious can mean we feel that we lack something. For example, you might not believe in yourself, you may feel that you don't have control of a situation, worry about their image, or you could even feel uneasy in certain social situations. If you want to progress your career, you can work on these things and develop yourself. Personal development can help you grow as a person and in your career.

The Individualist can aim for success in their career and head for their dream career, but there are some things you can do to improve your prospects and start striving towards that career:

- Spend some time working on yourself. Find out

what your problem is and what internal barriers are stopping you from moving on. Work on things like your self-confidence, your social ease and the way you feel about your self-image, in particular.

- Focus on your skills, especially your creative skills and think about how they can help you excel in your preferred career choice.
- Keep a personal growth journal. Set small goals and practice overcoming your barriers. For example, work on teamwork, putting yourself into uncomfortable social situations, or being comfortable with your image.
- Think about your future and consider different careers that may suit you, based on your preferences and skills. Don't be afraid to focus on your lifelong dream, even if it means it will be a journey for you. Plan ahead and make small steps towards achieving your dreams.

The main thing for *The Individualist* is to accept themselves and make small steps when making changes. *The Individualist* is also known as being *The*

Romantic, and this can fit in with their free-spirited nature and creative flair. Use your strengths and skills, and work on yourself, and you will achieve your dreams (Enneagram Type 4 - The Creative, 2020)[xxxiii].

Master your finances by honing your skills

The Individualist can certainly learn to master their finances effectively. Finances may not be your strength, but there are some simple things you can do to master them. Money isn't everything to you, and you appreciate other things in life like love, friendship and helping others. That doesn't mean you shouldn't have a financial plan and savings too, especially if you're a freelancer or sole trader.

If you want to master your finances, there are some things that you can do to manage your finances effectively:

- Create a personal budget and a business one if necessary. Ensure you detail all of your income and expenditure.

- Check your bank accounts daily.
- Monitor your spends and set goals – are you earning enough? Saving enough? Don't be afraid to push yourself – set acceptable, good and best goals.
- Write some financial goals – what do you want and what should save for in your future? Don't be afraid to seek advice and invest your savings in away that suits you. If you have any debts, make sure you write a plan to deal with this and think about how quickly you can get this done.
- Get thrifty! Think of some ways to save money, and other ways to make some extra cash too.

Finance is important for us all as we all need money to survive. Remember that there are lots of financial help out there to help you. This includes guidance online, accountants, bookkeepers and financial advisors too.

It's time to start and take your finances seriously. When you start to save, you can start to look at ways to invest and you might even start paying into a pension. All of these things will ensure success in the future.

Build emotional, mental, and physical health practices that work best for *The Individualist*

The Individualist can be emotional, and this is because of their insecurities. Their self-conscious issues can affect both their emotional and mental health, and this can have a detrimental affect. Fours can be quite negative, and they struggle to let go of the past. They can also long for things they don't have, and this takes over and they are unable to recognize the good things they have in their life.

For anyone, being aware of your issues is the first step to improving your health. You can improve your emotional and mental health which is to work on developing yourself and your mindset. Try reading some self-help books, enrolling in a self-confidence or self-esteem course, or get some cognitive behavioral therapy.

Physical health is just as important as mental and emotional health and it can actually improve mental health too. Exercise can help us to feel positive – it gives us the feel-good factor. Why not try something new?

- Dance fit/Zumba class. They can cater for all levels of fitness as there are different difficulty levels, but they are a great physical workout. They can make you good!
- Pilates class. Pilates class helps you work your core muscles and as your core gets stronger, your inner self will too.
- Box fit/boxercise. If dancing isn't your thing then you could try exercise that combines fitness and boxing. You use your arms in a boxing type style, but then you also use your legs too, for maximum impact.

Remember to seek advice from a qualified medical professional if you suffer from emotional, mental and physical health issues. If you are self-conscious or have low confidence/self-esteem, it can escalate, and this can affect your mental, physical and emotional health. We've talked about awareness and this is certainly the first step, but try writing down some goals – how do you want to act and feel? What would be ideal for you? It's important that you have some idea of what you want, and this applies to your emotional, mental and physical health, relationships and your career too.

Become a Leadership Rockstar with your Enneagram skillset

At their best, *The Individualist* express themselves well, and are profoundly creative. They feel inspired by others and can turn this inspiration into something positive and valuable. They love to start over or start something new and they are aware of their feelings, as they are on a journey to find their true self. They are strong, sensitive to others and have good intuition, which makes them effective leaders.

When leading others, *The Individualist* does not bark orders. They are self-aware and passionate, but their free-spirited nature and artistic attitude means that they sometimes get involved in themselves and what they are doing. This can mean they stray from their leading role. On the plus side, this means that they are great at leading a team of strong individuals who can speak their mind and use their initiative, but they might struggle to deal with those who need constant leadership and guidance.

The Individualist needs to work on their team working and team leadership skills, in order to excel as a leader. They must listen to their team, and not allow their self-consciousness and self-esteem issues get the better of them as this will affect their ability to lead and it can have a detrimental impact on the team.

The Individualist should embrace their creativity and open themselves up to their team, making sure they are honest and compassionate. They should practice spontaneity now and then and promote or encourage others to trust their intuitive side. Although they are not forceful or assertive, this may be something that they need to work on to move forward with their team.

In order to transform into a more effective leader, *The Individualist* should continue to self-improve. They should use their creativity to inspire others, and constantly work on their mindset. They should stay focused on transforming themselves and others into something of value and use their passion to drive others. To do this you should:

- Ensure you promote teamwork by holding team meetings or brainstorming meetings to discuss workload, working methods and new ideas. This can also show your team you're willing to listen to them.
- Be honest with your team. Honesty builds up trust and if you're not always good at leading or sharing, set out your expectations.
- Set team goals together so that everyone knows what they are doing.
- Use your creativity to inspire and motivate your team. For example, share your own ideas and encourage them to share theirs. *What about team building days, exercises or activities too?*
- Work and refine yourself and your own skills. This way you can lead by example. If your confidence is low, do something about it and show your team you have initiative and are

ready to face any issues.
- Make yourself open and approachable, so that your team feel like they can talk to you.

It may take some time for you to get used to leading others, but once you master the skills and mindset, you will be an awesome leader.

Top Tips to Boost your efficiency through problem-solving methods that work for you

The Individualist is able to problem solve already, but there are ways they can boost their efficiency when doing this. Their lack of self-esteem and self-conscious feelings can cloud their judgement when problem solving. *The Individualist* sometimes prefers lone working too, but they need to find a way to trust others as well as themselves. This will help to become a more efficient problem solver.

To improve their efficiency, *The Individualist* should:

- Work on their teamworking skills and building up

trust with others. Don't be afraid to talk to others and problem solve together. Take into account what other people say and make sure you keep a clear head so that you can solve problems objectively.

- Work on your self-esteem and self-consciousness. This can be a huge barrier and it can hold you back. If you start to believe in yourself, other people will believe in you and this will boost how you feel. When we feel good and our confidence grows, we are able to think in a more logical and accurate way, as well being able to make well-informed decisions.
- Follow a problem-solving 5-step structure. You can do this in a group or as an individual and as you're a creative person, you should use that to inspire and motivate yourself and others – thinking of something different and innovative ways to solve a problem is a positive thing:

1. Analyze the problem and its causes. Work out your end goal.
2. Brainstorm alternative solutions or

interventions that will help you achieve that end goal.

3. Evaluate the possibilities and choose the most effective solution.
4. Plan and implement your solution strategy.
5. Monitor and assess its overall effectiveness.

- Open communication channels and listen to others when it comes to identifying problems, solving problems and monitoring their effectiveness. Having an open mind and being open to suggestions from others can be a crucial part of the process as we all have different ideas and specialize in different things.

The biggest challenge for you when solving problems is your preference to work alone as this is a difficult habit for you to break. This is something you should work on. Ensure you research well, consult with others, and use your problem-solving structure or formula when searching for solutions. Learning to build trust with others can help you grow as a person too, as everything we experience is a learning curve. Thinking differently and learning to recognize your own achievements and other's achievements will only help you feel inspired and be inspiring to others. This will mean you are likely to change your mindset, and the way you both think of and approach problems.

Discover a path to spirituality that works best for your personality type

The Individualist can discover a path to spirituality and this will help them to work through their self-consciousness and self-esteem issues. There are many benefits to being spiritual, as it can help you to automatically form positive think patterns and adopt a more positive outlook and mindset. *The Individualist* can be a naturally negative thinker, so spirituality will certainly be beneficial to you.

The Individualist can be more spiritual by:

- Taking time to relax and reflect.
- Work through your own negative thoughts. Write them down and then write a response to your feeling or action. *How should you have reacted*

to the problem?
- Visualize the ideal you. *How would you act, feel or behave? What would you be like if you were your ideal self? What would you change?*
- Change the way you respond when negative things happen. Think of them as a learning curve and evaluate how the whole situation could be improved. *What would you do differently? How do you wish you had handled the situation? What would you change next time?*

The Individualist often stresses about their self-image and this can hold them back. If you want to improve how you feel about your own self image, you can take action. First, you should be kind to yourself. Stay calm and take a more objective view of yourself, by viewing yourself from an outside perspective. Imagine you're assessing someone else, and not yourself... *Would you be as harsh?* Secondly, you need to stop comparing yourself to others. Everyone is different and we all have different skills, qualities and abilities that define us. Be who you want to be, and don't try to become like another person. It's time to accept yourself and transform yourself into the person you are and want to be. Being true to yourself will make you happy!

You can improve how you feel about yourself by being more spiritual and for *The Individualist* you might like to try confidence building guided meditations, or even hypnosis. Not everyone is susceptible to hypnosis, but it can have positive effects when it comes to increasing self-confidence, building self-awareness, being less self-conscious and changing your negative thought patterns into positives. Don't rule it out without giving it a try – you might enjoy it!

Connect the dots to create a vision for progress and growth

If your dominant personality is *The Individualist,* then personal growth is important to help develop your personality type. To connect the dots and fulfill your vision, we should look at the 9 levels of development for this particular personality type. You should be aiming for healthy levels, 1-3. Average levels are 4-6, but if you find yourself dropping to level 6, you need to really focus on making steady improvements. If your levels are unhealthy (levels 7-9), action is needed now, and you may even need extra support from a medical professional. Keep an eye on your levels, because it's important to monitor them.

Healthy levels

Level 1 – This is *The Individualist* at their very best. They are all about being creative and expressing themselves through a creative, expressive or artistic means. At this level, they are optimistic people who transform their experiences into something positive, regardless of whether they are positive or negative. Confidence is at a healthy level and this makes a world of difference.

Level 2 – At level 2, *The Individualist* is sensitive, gentle and shows compassion to others. They are very self-aware, self-reflective and are on a journey of self-discovery. They have good intuition and can mostly identify and manage their own feelings, impulses and actions. Their level of awareness is strong, and this means they are able to work on any negative feelings like lack of self-esteem and self-consciousness.

Level 3 – At level 3, *The Individualist* is serious, but they are unique and can also be funny. They are strong, emotionally, but they sometimes have an atypical view of life and their self. They are honest, true to themselves, and they are highly personal and individualistic.

Average levels
Level 4 – At level 4, *The Individualist* is romantic and artistic, and they use this to shape the direction they take in their life. They are very passionate and have a creative imagination. They have strong personal feelings that they attempt to prolong, but their aim is to create a visual and beautiful environment.

Level 5 – *The Individualist* at this level can be spontaneous. They are in touch with their feelings, but they can be hypersensitive as they start to take everything personally. This often results in moody and introverted behavior, and they become absorbed only in themselves. Self-consciousness is starting to break through at this stage, and they can become withdrawn.

Level 6 – When at level 6, *The Individualist* thinks they are different to others. They are dreamers and sensual, but this sometimes suggests that they live in a fantasy world. They feel a lot of self-pity, and they get jealous of others. This means they can overindulge due to feelings of sadness. This often leads to them being impractical and unproductive.

Unhealthy levels

Level 7 – *The Individualist* can start to feel angry. They are ashamed of themselves, and generally tired which makes it difficult to function effectively. They are loners and keep themselves separate from others. They emotionally protect themselves from others and are prone to depression.

Level 8 – At this level, *The Individualist* feels self-hatred and loathing, and they suffer with morbid thoughts. They are quick to blame others for any wrong-doings, and they have a habit of pushing away those who are trying to help them. They feel contempt for themselves and suffer with delusions too. Confidence is really low, but this is escalating and it's difficult to see a way forward.

Level 9 – This is the lowest level and at level 9. *The Individualist* is often feeling hopeless and depressed at this stage. This can lead to desperate measures in which they start to participate in destructive behavior. This can include things like an emotional breakdown, substance misuse, and sometimes feelings of suicide. This can lead to narcissistic personality disorders in some cases, if they don't get help.

If you are *The Individualist,* you need to ensure that you are self-aware and keep track of what level you're at. If you find yourself in the unhealthy levels, the sooner you get help, the better. You should certainly seek professional medical advice and deal with any issues in the correct way, that's most effective for you. If you are at average or healthy levels, you should still look at different ways to develop and improve. Write yourself some goals, and a future plan. Don't forget to create smaller steps so you can map out your growth plan and monitor your progress as this is the best way to ensure success. (The Enneagram Institute, 2020)[xxxiv]

Affirmations for *The Individualist*

I am a significant for the success of the team and their opinions or contributions count.

I am confident in my own abilities and the abilities of others.

I am successful, creative and expressive. This means I can achieve anything.

Chapter 6

Type Five: The Investigator

Do you often find yourself alone, but it doesn't worry you, because you prefer it? The Investigator is generally perceptive, but they are often a loner and can be very secretive. They have an intense and curious personality and strive for innovation. They are visionaries and are great at developing strategies and focusing on ideas. Let's find out more about personality type 5: The Investigator and how we can develop it.

Introduction to *The Investigator:*

The Investigator is alert and inventive. Their independent and insightful nature drives them in everything they do. They can develop complex ideas and have a strong skillset, yet they can become detached from others. Type fives are easily distracted, and they can be eccentric and intense, which often leads them to isolate themselves. Their future plans and visions only demonstrate their ability to see a refreshing and innovative future, but they need to be careful as they often preoccupy themselves with their thoughts.

The Investigator often wants to know what, or why something has happened. It's their life's mission to search for answers as they continuously ask questions and have a strong need for the truth. They want to know the most scientific and the most spiritual thing and investigate concepts and ideas that shape the world and everything in it. They want to know everything in depth and prefer facts rather than opinions. Gaining insight and the truth is important to them!

PROFILE: *The Investigator*

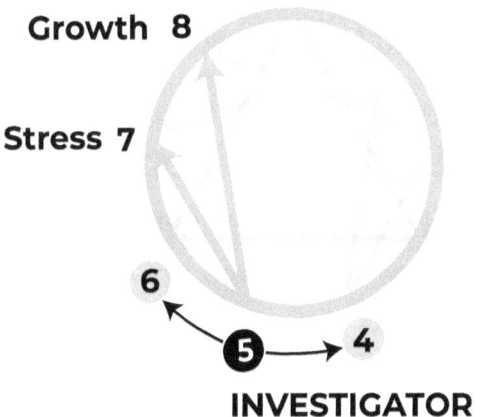

INVESTIGATOR

Key Desire: They long to believe they are capable and competent people, in order to achieve success.

Key Fear: They fear being incapable. They want to be helpful and useful, so they don't want to fail at this.

Wings possibilities: If you work well independently, and have an eye for the small details, you could be a type five with a four-wing and this would suggest that you are the *The Iconoclast*. If you're type five with a six-wing, you could be *The Problem-solver.*

Five with a four-wing: *If you have a four-wing, you are The Iconoclast.* This means you are attentive and well-focused, as well being a creative thinker. Sometimes, you can be overly sensitive, so try not to take things to heart or allow your sensitivity to prevent you from getting what you want in life *(Enneagram Type 5w4 - The Philosopher, 2020)*[xxxv].

Five with a six-wing: *If you have a six-wing, you are The Problem-solver.* You are great at solving complex problems, and during a time of crisis, you are great remaining calm and collected. Sometimes you are extremely private and cold towards others, and this can affect your relationships – so this is something to be aware of *(Enneagram Type 5w6 - The Troubleshooter, 2020)*[xxxvi].

Key motivations: *The Investigator* longs to hold a wide range of knowledge and understanding. They aim to figure out the world, so they are driven by this need to research and seek out answers. Their possession of knowledge is important as they want to understand their environment. They believe knowledge is power and know how to defend themselves against anything that threatens that environment.

Strengths: *The Investigator* is innovative and

perceptive. They learn from their experiences and enjoy their search for answers. They value knowledge, education and experience, and enjoy working for a better future. They are excellent at developing strategies and enjoy theoretical explanations and ideas. They are great thinkers and spend time observing and contemplating events or findings.

Stress points and Growth:

As they move into the path of disintegration (stress) towards number 7, a Type Five can become manic and sporadic. Following the arrow of integration (growth) towards number 8, can mean their confidence increases and they become an authoritative figure (The Enneagram Institute, 2020)[xxxvii].

How *The Investigator* can hack their own success?

The Investigator can hack their own success easily as they already have the knowledge they need to achieve their dreams. They are relentless learners with a 'never give up' attitude. They have crucial, high-level thinking skills that allow them to identify, observe and contemplate, so they are excellent problem solvers.

Fives are great at immersing themselves into situations and they value learning, education and knowledge, but they prefer to work alone and can be quite secretive when working in a team. They have deep-rooted insecurities that can also hold them back, but at their best, *The Investigator* can control these things. As they are committed to proving themselves competent and able, they can easily hack their own success by:

- Working on their trust issues.
- Improving their teamworking skills.
- Spending some time on their personal development to help work through their insecurities. Often, this is something simple like improving self-esteem, or taking a more positive approach and annihilating the negative thinking patterns that sometimes take over in our mind.

To hack your success, you should set yourself some success goals for the future and use your investigative skills to find out what you need to work on to get there. Dig deep and ask yourself, *what makes me successful?* Because we all have a different idea of what success is – it's something different for everyone.

Another way to hack your success is to make lists of the skills and qualities you already have, and the skills and qualities you would like to improve. Give a reason why you want to improve or develop specific skills and qualities, as the *'why'* is what motivates us.

Self-care is so important if you want to be successful. Make sure that you spend time every day reflecting on the things you did well. We are quick to judge the things we did wrong and scold ourselves for it, so from now on, reflect on the things you do that are positive.

Hacking your own success is personal to you. Create a success plan for yourself and use your goals that we talked about earlier. Make sure you monitor progress as *The Investigator* struggles to recognize their own achievements. You should also create some affirmations that are meaningful to you; as you long to be competent and capable, so you need to start believing this.

Using the enneagram to achieve self-improvement

If you want to improve yourself, there are certainly areas that are key to maintaining your own healthy levels. The main thing for you is recognizing the positive things about yourself, and that includes your abilities, personal qualities and skills. Your fear is not being useful and helpful, but in order to improve, you need to work on your fears and get to the root of any issues.

If you're *The Investigator* and you want to improve yourself, you should focus on your personal fears. You can do this by:

- Write a list of what personal improvements you would like to make to your self.
- Think about what fears stem from them – *why do you want to make these improvements?*
- Do what you do best! Think, reflect, assess and contemplate your fears. *What's the worst that*

can happen in relation to your fear? What's the best positive outcome?
- Mark down your achievements and be proud. Ensure you celebrate your wins and tick off your personal improvements.

The Investigator has some unique skills and qualities but often struggles to believe in themselves. Increasing your self-belief is important for your personal development too. Try reading some enlightening self-help books or enrol in a personal development course.

Strengthening Relationships – tapping into your own strengths

The Investigator is one of the most introverted personality types which means forming relationships is not easy for them. With that in mind, if you are type five, you need time to build trust with others and can often feel overwhelmed.

You enjoy time alone to think and process information,

and you hate feeling like others are making demands. This is sometimes difficult for the people in your life. You have many positive things to bring to a relationship as you are a great thinker and listener. You do need to ensure you don't spend your time overthinking and analyzing because this can actually prevent you from getting on in your life. The investigator always wants more and wants to do better, so this drives them in life.

Fives can come across as being distant, but this is mostly because they don't want to get hurt. This doesn't mean they are not capable of love, but relationships tend to disrupt their flow. For example if they form a friendship, they have to take time to be a friend, and if they have a partner or spouse, they have to put time and effort into the relationship, which again, disrupts the things they usually do. They often avoid building close relationships because of these feelings but being a loner can just make social interactions and situations worse.

Before forming and strengthening relationships, *The Investigator* should work on themselves. They need to build their confidence, confront their trust issues, and involve themselves in social situations that can sometimes make them feel uncomfortable.

If you truly want to strengthen relationships, you need to be honest with the people you are in a relationship with. This can be family, friends, partners and even work colleagues, neighbours or acquaintances. Let your family and friends know that you are aware of your relationship issues and will make a conscious effort to maintain your relationships. For instance, agree to visit close family members once each week, attend their celebration event you were thinking about avoiding, and go for coffee with your friends once each month. Make a commitment or pledge to make this effort.

The Investigator is used to being alone, and this is a hard habit to break but people will understand. Don't be afraid to set boundaries when you need your space but ensure you are also there for the people that you love. Relationships are not one-sided, and others like to see emotion and vulnerability. This may take some time for you, because of your trust issues but you will get there

– don't give up! (Relationship Type 5 with Type 5 — The Enneagram Institute, 2020)[xxxviii].

Achieving your career potential

For *The Investigator,* it's particularly important to do what you love. It can be difficult for you as an introvert to participate in social events, and although we all need to step out of our comfort zone, choose a job you love, that suits your personality type.

To achieve your career potential, you really need to consider your career options. There's no doubt that you're a great thinker, researcher and assessor, so there are many options for you. Problem solving is one of your key skills, because you can assess things in a logical, objective way. You are good at creating strategies, writing policies, and helping businesses move forward through innovation. Research roles and business solutions would be ideal career opportunities for you to pursue, but you are creative too, so don't rule anything out until you are certain of what you want to do.

The Investigator definitely prefers to work alone, and there's a chance that you do not have great teamworking skills as you can be quite secretive. If you need to get ahead in your career, you should:

- List your strengths and figure out what path you want to take.
- Work on your soft skills, like presentation skills, effective teamworking, organizational techniques would be great for *The Investigator*.
- Keep a confidence journal to monitor your journey when increasing your confidence.
- Create your career goals and use checklists to list the things you need to do, in order to achieve these goals.

The main thing for *The Investigator* is to find a career that they love, that appeals to them. Keep monitoring your personal growth as well as your career plans. Be careful, as it's important you don't become too overwhelmed, so take small steps when making personal changes.

Master your finances by honing your skills

The Investigator is usually good at managing their finances. They think about every purchase and spend and contemplate it. You can develop your skills further and learn to master your finances. To do this, you should:

- Create a budget that includes all income and expenditure.
- Assess your spends carefully – *Do you want the item? Do you need the item? Can you afford it?*
- Set financial targets and make sure they are SMART.
- You're already quite thrifty with your money, so why not get some financial advice, to see if you can make any savings or invest.

As you are a great thinker, and you do your research, you have strong skills that you could use to master your finances. You should look at securing your money for the future too!
(Enneagram Type 5 - The Thinker, 2020)[xxxix].

Build emotional, mental, and physical health practices that work best for *The Investigator*

The Individualist can be intense. As mentioned earlier in this chapter, they struggle to see their own worth and this lowers their self-esteem. Fives enjoy being alone, but if they are in the wrong frame of mind, this can actually make things worse for them.

As you are a loner and most fives prefer it that way, it's important that they manage their own mental, emotional and physical health practices effectively and become aware of any triggers.

You have some great skills that you can use to self-manage your emotions. Remember, an emotion is a feeling and we still have a choice – we choose what action to take as a result of how we feel. You are excellent at problem solving and analyzing, so the first step is acknowledging your emotion and analyzing it, so that you can get to its root cause. When you do, treat it as a problem and figure out a solution.

When we feel emotion, it's a good idea to talk about it as, if we struggle to cope with our emotions, it can lead to mental health issues. If you can't talk about it, due to your trust and confidence issues then there are some things you can do to ease that. Ultimately, you should have at least one person you can talk to whether this be a counsellor, a family member or a friend. If you feel like that's not possible for you at this time, you could try keeping a gratitude journal. This is a journal in which you write down what you are grateful for. Write down positive things in this every night but reflect on this every morning so you feel motivated. When things seem emotionally challenging, you should always remember the things you are thankful for. Regardless of this advice, you do need to be prepared to seek professional or medical advice if your emotions or mental state deteriorates. Staying aware can help you decide then that's possible.

Your lack of confidence and fear of failing can also affect your mental health. Use your gratitude journal to be thankful of your learning and experiences. You know the value of knowledge, so celebrate that and know that if it makes you feel good, that's okay. Things like exposure therapy, CBT, and mindfulness can help you grow your confidence. You can also read a range of self-help books too!

Improving your physical health can really help you to improve your feel-good factor. Ideal exercises for *The Investigator* are:

- Running. Running is great as you can do this alone. It can help you to think better.
- Biking. Biking is great physical exercise that works many parts of your body. You can also do this at a level.
- Yoga. Yoga is a great exercise for you because it's relaxing, but it also keeps you supple. The breathing exercises are good calming techniques.

Looking after your emotional and physical needs are key. This can be tricky when you are *The Investigator,* but provided that you remain self-aware and honest with yourself it can be self-managed. If you feel good, it can mean you are generally more positive, and this has numerous benefits. Keep building your confidence and self-worth, and purposely put yourself in those uncomfortable situations. Life is challenging so sometimes if we want to move up or on, we have to step out of our comfort zone. Just remember to seek advice from a qualified medical professional if you suffer from emotional, mental and physical health issues, and you feel that those have escalated.

Become a Leadership Rockstar with your Enneagram skillset

At their best, *The Investigator* can be a great leader. As they have strong thinking, researching and analyzing skills, they can lead others well through change. They do prefer to work alone, but they are natural visionaries and they easily inspire others with their innovative attitude. They are open minded and perceptive, and once they master their team working skills, they can become very effective and efficient leaders.

A good leader listens to their team, leads by example,

and can see the value in others and themselves. These are skills that you may need to tweak or master. You have excellent skills at managing projects as you are great at developing ideas and solving any problems that stand in your way. You are good at connecting the dots and through your observations you can create synergy when completing work tasks.

In order to transform into a more effective leader, *The Investigator* needs to improve some of their skills. They need to ensure they maintain a positive frame of mind and stay focused. It's important to remember that teamwork is important. Use your innovative ideas to lead your team:

- Promote positive teamwork by holding team meetings or brainstorming meetings to discuss workload, working methods and new ideas. This can also show your team you're willing to listen to them. Your leadership style may be to allow your team to take ownership of their work and that's fine,
- Set clear goals for the team together, so that

everyone can take ownership, and everyone knows what they should be doing.
- Use your perception and observation skills to help your team lead effectively and help them develop their own careers through supervisions, appraisals and performance reviews. This will help them maintain their motivations.
- Make yourself open and approachable, so that your team feel like they can talk to you.

Leadership may not be something you find easy, but your skillset show that this is something you can be really good at. Your knowledge, understanding and insight are inspiring to others and they will be valued by your employer. Take a team leading training course if you need some extra help at developing this skill. You are independent and you can teach your team to be the same, just let your confidence shine too – you have so much to offer as a leader!

Top Tips to Boost your efficiency through problem-solving methods that work for you

For *The Investigator,* problem-solving comes easily to you. That's because (as we've discussed earlier) you are excellent at researching, observing and assessing problems, and you use your knowledge, skills and experience to help you deal with them. To boost your problem-solving methods, you could focus on working in a team as we often solve problems more effectively if we work with others – this will be a great learning curve for you and for the others in your team.

To improve their efficiency, *The Investigator* should:

- Focus on their listening and communication skills. Listen to others and communicate your own ideas clearly, explaining the problem or possible solutions.
- You have good problem-solving skills and you should be confident in them. Ensure that you value yourself, your experience and your intuition.
- Use your strengths in observing, thinking and assessing to resolve any issues. Remember to be objective.

- Follow a problem-solving structure. Brainstorm the problem and possible solutions, analyze the possible solutions, and write clear goals that will offer the best solution. Ensure you list some smaller steps to help you focus on achieving your end goal but stay motivated at the same time.
- Believe in your solutions and overcome any barriers in your way. Have a back-up plan, in case it doesn't work, but keep a clear head and don't be afraid to seek advice or change your strategy.
- Ensure you learn by your experiences. Sometimes we solve problems through trial and error. Discuss what did or didn't work with your team and keep striving for your end goal. Accept that things don't always go to plan, but don't give up.

When you're used to working alone, it can be challenging to start working in a team to solve problems but stick with it and you'll get it. You may need to start changing the way you think as you mustn't fear failure or allow situations to overwhelm you. Ask for advice if you need it and keep an open mind!

Discover a path to spirituality that works best for your personality type

For *The Investigator,* they can use spirituality to allow them to clear their mind, forgive themselves and work on their self-confidence. It's not always easy to adopt this, but because you like to learn and absorb knowledge, it could be easier than you think – you've just got to believe you can do it.

The Investigator can be more spiritual by:

- Gaining insight through reading self-help books.
- Taking time reflect by trying some breathing activities to help you relax and maintain a clear mind.
- Assess your negative thoughts logically. Write them down, write how you feel and write a solution – you're good at working through problems. Think about your ideal thought or

action, and how you should've responded. *What would you change?*
- Try breathing exercises and meditations that can help with confidence and spirituality.

The Investigator often has many insecurities and spirituality can help them deal with this. Personal development can really help you grow as a person and you need to learn the value of yourself and build your confidence. Spirituality can help you to create balance. You could burn some sage to cleanse your space or use aromatherapy to help you relax and alter your mood. As you enjoy time alone to think, aromatherapy can be a great touch as a thinker is often open to spirituality. Try it! It could really help to boost your confidence and prevent the negative thoughts that sometimes swirl in your head. *The Investigator* often finds other people draining but being spiritual can actually help you increase your energy levels.

Connect the dots to create a vision for progress and growth

If your dominant personality is *The Investigator,* your personal growth journey is about to begin and it's important to remember you're not alone. To connect the dots and fulfill your vision, we should look at the 9 levels of development for this particular personality type. You should always strive for healthy levels, 1-3. Average levels are 4-6, but if you find yourself dropping to level 6, you need to really focus on making steady improvements. If your levels are unhealthy (levels 7-9), action is needed now, and you may even need extra support from a medical professional. Remember it's important to monitor your levels.

Healthy levels
Level 1 – This is *The Investigator* at their very best and they are awesome! They have a strong and in-depth comprehension of the world and visualize the future. They take everything in their stride and within context and remain very open minded. They are innovative and perceptive, and love to find new ways of working or doing things.

Level 2 – At level 2, *The Investigator* observes everything. They have an aptitude for gaining insight and this shapes their visions for the future and gives them ideas. They are curious, intelligent and alert, and they notice every detail. They have excellent concentration levels which allows them to solve problems, research and analyze well.

Level 3 – At level 3, *The Investigator* masters everything. Knowledge excites them and they strive to become an expert in things that interest them. They are original but enjoy being independent and search for value in everything they do. They are inventive and strive for something new. They love to learn new skills and gain insight through their experiences.

Average levels

Level 4 – At level 4, *The Investigator* starts to improve and conceptualize everything before they act. They want everything to be perfect and try to work this out in their mind. They love to specialize in specific topics and pass themselves off as an intellectual. They challenge ways of doing things and enjoy gathering evidence and resources to acquire new techniques.

Level 5 – *The Investigator* starts to be detached from practicality. They become preoccupied with their own interpretations and visions, and this takes over reality. They can start to become fascinated with disturbing or dark elements, as they become more involved with complicated idea and imaginary fantasy worlds. They try to separate themselves often from others.

Level 6 – When at level 6, *The Investigator* can become cynical, argumentative and antagonistic. They don't like anyone or anything interfering in their person world and vision, and they can form radical views.

Unhealthy levels

Level 7 – *The Investigator* often becomes reclusive at this level. They are eccentric and isolated in their own reality, which makes them fearful. This can result in them suffering with feelings of aggression and they can start to show signs of being unstable. They reject the help of others and often avoid social attachments.

Level 8 – At this level, *The Investigator* is starting to be obsessed and could possibly be scaring themselves with their ideas at this time. They can be delirious and start to develop phobias. This is not a good place and they need to accept at this stage that they need help.

Level 9 – This is the lowest level and at level 9. *The Investigator* is on a downwards spiral and is becoming deranged. They are self-destructive and can show schizophrenic overtones. They will certainly be displaying signs of personality disorders and need immediate professional help. They could be so low, they are thinking of suicide and suffering from a psychotic break. Reality is far away from them right now!

If someone is *The Investigator* , they can be a spectacular person when their levels are healthy, but they do have to monitor their need for isolation, because it means they separate themselves from help and support from others. The healthy levels are a great place to be, and you should form your personal growth plan so that it plays to the strengths of your personality – there certainly are many. You must be honest with yourself and others, and keep working on your self-esteem and social skills. If you find yourself straying towards the unhealthy levels, you should consider seeking advice from a qualified medical professional. Awareness, acceptance and communication skills are essential for you and your future. (The Enneagram Institute, 2020)[xl]

Affirmations for *The Investigator*

I am smart and confident in myself and my own abilities.

I am a team player and can trust other people who have earned it.

I am changing for the better, but because I am finally being myself, I am growing into the person I love.

DID YOU ENJOY THIS BOOK?

We would truly appreciate if you could leave a review on Amazon. We are an independent publishing company and read each and every review!

amazon
★★★★★

Chapter 7

Type Six: The Loyalist

Can you foresee problems before they happen? If you can, and you are concerned for yourself and others, as well as being responsible and trustworthy then you could be *The Loyalist*. They are very committed, loyal and hard working but they can also be anxious. They can sometimes be defensive and suspicious, but they are very security orientated and focused are focused problem-solvers.

Introduction to *The Loyalist*:

The Loyalist lives by their label as they are very loyal to their friends, systems and beliefs. They are defensive of friends, family and community, more so than they are of themselves. They are very determined to solve problems, and often help to create, develop and maintain structures. If you're a six, you probably enjoy the company of others and sometimes they validate you. You feel you must work with others and therefore, you do what you can to hold on to them. Sixes can suffer with anxiety and this can sometimes escalate, so it's important that they deal with this.

The Loyalist tends to worry a lot about everything as they don't always have confidence when it comes to making judgements. They try to consult their inner self for guidance, but they struggle to truly connect with it. Sixes endeavor to build networks because belief isn't always easy for them. Once they meet someone, they try to keep their connections. They also want to feel purpose in their life too. Generally, *The Loyalist* is intelligent, but sometimes, self-doubt holds them back.

PROFILE: *The Loyalist*

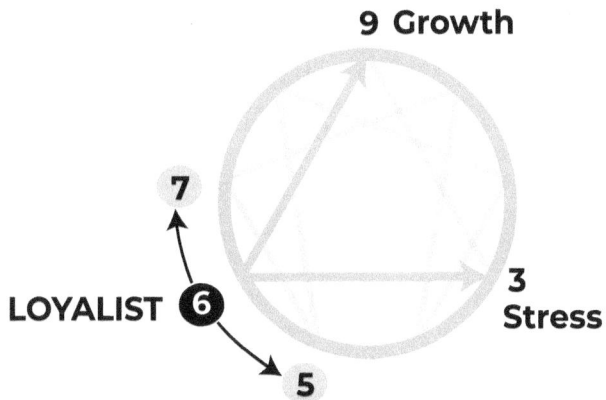

Key Desire: They long for security and like to have support from others as this boosts them.

Key Fear: Sixes fear being without support and this often includes a network of people that they can go to for help and guidance. Their biggest fear is not having this and not having access to guidance.

Wings possibilities: If you're practical and efficient then you could have a five-wing this would suggest that you are *The Defender.* If you're sociable and always honor your commitments then you could have a seven-wing, and in that case, you are *The Buddy.*

Six with a five-wing: If you have a five-wing, you're

The Defender. You have a passion for knowledge and you're a great problem-solver. You work alone, but you struggle to control your negative thinking patterns which is something you should work on. (Enneagram Type 6w5 - The Guardian, 2020)[xli].

Six with a seven-wing: If you have a seven-wing, you are *The Buddy.* That means you care deeply for others, and you are naturally sociable. You take your commitments and any promises you make, seriously but when it comes to yourself, you sometimes struggle to make decisions that affect your life (Enneagram Type 6w7 - The Confidant, 2020)[xlii].

Key motivations: Reassurance goes a long way with sixes, and this tends to motivate them. They like gratification and for a support network that will clarify that 'everything will be okay', so they are often motivated by others. They like to feel safe and secure, and if they feel that others have their back, they can excel in everything they do. They can be valuable and logical problem solvers because of their love to help others – this also motivates them.

Strengths: *The Loyalist* is a people person who is great at attracting others, and once they build up a relationship of trust, they defend others. They are good at taking responsibility and their strength is in their problem-solving abilities. They are good at supporting others and are great at building and facilitating that type of environment with others.

Stress points and Growth:

As they move into the path of disintegration (stress) towards number 3, type Six can become arrogant and very competitive. Following the arrow of integration (growth) towards number 9, a fearful type Six can become hopeful and more relaxed too (The Enneagram Institute, 2020)[xliii].

How *The Loyalist* can hack their own success

You are already successful or heading in that direction, but sometimes your self-doubt clouds that, and you don't see it. There are ways you can hack your success and start to build up that self-belief.

Sixes are great people, who attract other people because it's in their nature. They defend others and build communities, and they can use their strength to hack their success:

- The first thing you need to do to hack your success, is work on your anxiety issues.
- Learn how to use your own skills to justify your decisions, rather than needing clarification from others. It's fine to have a support network, but you need to build your confidence in your own decisions too, so that you can grab that success with both hands.
- Use your skills of building up a strong support network, and ensure you have someone to talk to who is kind and understanding. We all need a confidante from time to time.
- Take a time-out. Any parent knows the importance of a time-out, and sometimes we need that time to breathe and soak in the information. It can help to clear our head. If we clear out mind, it can help us to hack our own success. You could even use your time to exercise, as this can certainly clear your mind and help you become more motivated.
- Do something every day that makes you happy.

Being happy is what we all need in our life as it gives us a positive outlook. Laughing is also good for you and it can improve your anxiety too.

It's always good to set yourself goals that you can tick off. You can also create a bucket list for success too. Think about what success is to you. Consider the skills and qualities you already have and those you would like to improve. Set your goals to success based on what you really want – this may need to spend some time thinking about this – *What do you really want?* Try writing a letter from your future self as this can help you to achieve your goals. What will you be doing next year, in 5 or 10 years? You can then figure out what you need to do to become that person.

For *The Loyalist,* self-care should be at the top of your list. You shouldn't allow your anxiety to escalate as you will start to be suspicious of others, and this can damage your relationships.

Self-care is so important if you want to be successful. It's important that you take time to work on yourself. It can help you to work out those anxiety triggers that sometimes hold you back. Something like laughter yoga can be very beneficial to *The Loyalist.*

Hacking your own success can be done if you make a plan of action that you believe in. You can use your goals to do this, but ensure you are logical, and you should plan keeping in mind your own self-care too. Self-belief is a big thing for you, so work on your anxiety and its triggers. It's time to start believing!

Using the enneagram to achieve self-improvement

If you want to improve yourself, you need to reach and maintain the healthy levels within your personality. The key thing for you is to work on your anxiety, as you are in danger of letting this hold you back (if it isn't doing so already). Being anxious is not usual but learning to cope with it can improve many things in your life. Your fear is not having a supportive network of people around you, and this is partly because you need people to talk to and express yourself, and you also need to be reassured.

If you're *The Loyalist* and you want to improve yourself, you should focus on dealing and coping with your anxiety, so that you can create a more positive mindset:

- Write down any triggers or causes when it comes to your anxiety.
- Keep a mood journal and write down the different moods you experience throughout the day. If you notice that a particular task or event makes you happy, note it down. Do the same thing if something stresses you out or upsets you.
- Another good way to improve yourself is to eat better and drink plenty of water. Eating healthy snacks can have a more positive impact on our body than eating sugary or salty snacks. Increasing water intake keeps us thinking straight as hydration is important to keep us functioning effectively.
- Create a vision board of what you want in life and your goals, to keep you motivated. Remind yourself of what you want every day.

The Loyalist has many skills and qualities, but they can still improve themselves. If you learn to manage your anxiety and maintain a positive outlook, you will see vast improvements. Looking after yourself is the key to self-improvement.

Strengthening Relationships – tapping into your own strengths

The Loyalist is committed, engaging and responsible. They like to be secure, and they enjoy being within a network of people. They are trusting and independent yet coordinated and orientated towards others. They enjoy helping others and demonstrate courage. Being able to self-affirm helps *The Loyalist* develop their confidence as they truly start to believe in themselves rather than others. They can certainly be a great person when it comes to relationships as they have so many qualities.

Sixes enjoy being with others, as they enjoy being within a network of people and trust is very important to them. They like to build strong bonds, and have a good sense of humor, so it's great if the person who they have a relationship has one too as it helps strengthen their connection rapidly. Sixes are great at supporting partners, friends, family and colleagues and are great at sharing secrets and values with those they feel close to. They can have fun, but also enjoy intellectual conversations that stimulate their mind.

When at a healthy level, sixes are happy and supportive. They are protective of others and provide security, but this is when they need to maintain those healthy levels as they can feel doubt and suspicions, which can take over and then shroud their rationality. They are sensitive souls, but sometimes struggle to talk about their feelings. This is something that a six should work on because they need to learn to process their feelings, thoughts and actions in a rational way – this is important for their own happiness.

Before forming and strengthening relationships, *The Loyalist* should work on building their own confidence. Sometimes, they can react in a negative way and as they fear having nobody to turn to, falling out with another person can hit them hard. They can be impulsive, not think out a situation and this often blows a situation out of proportion. When this escalates, a six can start to blame other people and their anxiety increases. As they take everything in a serious way, they can feel betrayed by a non-serious event and they can struggle to regain trust in such instances. Because trust is so important to a six, this can damage their relationship.

If sixes want to strengthen relationships, it's important to work on controlling their anxious thoughts. As *The Loyalist* can be a pessimist, it's important that you work on having a more positive outlook. A six has a high level of self-doubt and are often filled with insecurities, so sometimes they don't trust their own decision-making skills – in fact they fear it. This doesn't help when it comes to a relationship, because your family, partner, colleagues and friends shouldn't have to intervene in every decision you make. A relationship should always be two-sided, and both parties need to contribute. If you strengthen your ability to make confident, well-thought-out decisions, it will only improve your relationships. Another thing you should work on to strengthen your relationships, are trust and insecurity issues. This can make you deceptive, clingy, and remember, false accusations lead to conflict. If you overcome your security issues and work on conquering your feelings towards trust, you will create and maintain positive, healthy relationships. There's no doubt that trust is earned over time, however, we have to accept that we can't completely protect ourselves or others from being let down from time to time. This happens in life and we have to learn to deal with these things and move on! (Relationship Type 6 with Type 6 — The Enneagram Institute, 2020)[xliv]

Achieving your career potential

There are many career opportunities for *The Loyalist*. You are able to thrive in organizations that value their employee's abilities and offer job security, because you feel safe. There's nothing wrong with looking for a secure job and this has many benefits. If that's what you want, keep searching for that ideal job that promises security.

The Loyalist works well with others. They are supportive and work best when they have a support network. They are great at building networks of support and this can help to motivate the team. This is a strength you can take to any job role. They are a people person, and others find it easy to connect and confide in them. Sixes likes to feel valuable and they can be direct, which is often appreciated amongst the team as they do this in a professional way. They are also pragmatic, hardworking and committed to their team and any project they are tasked with. All of these skills are an asset to you!

If you want to achieve your career potential, you need to think about things you need to improve. You worry about not making the right decisions, but sometimes the worry overwhelms you. You can:

- Face your anxieties and find out your triggers.
- Work on your confidence and self-belief. You can enrol on some online courses or read self-help books. Start to apply them to the workplace.

The Loyalist takes everything to heart and can be quite defensive. They sometimes see criticism as a personal attack, rather than taking it in the context it's meant in. Sometimes, in an unstable environment you don't perform your best, but you don't understand that this could prevent you from progressing. You need to show people how valuable you are and what they would be missing if they lost you. You also need to take advantage of every experience you are offered, as it could contribute to your future – you might even learn something new. To improve, you can:

- Stop reacting to criticism negatively. Reprogram the way you think and start to think differently. Step away and take an outside point of view, this will help you assess the situation in an objective way. Remember that criticism can help us improve.
- Work on your mindset, and always go out of your way to be the best they can be. Use your skills effectively and view everything as a learning curve.

Ideal careers for *The Loyalist* could be in a legal or nursing profession. They also work well in an office or financial environment and can also be great leaders. Keep working hard and stop worrying about making an incorrect decision – give yourself a break, we're only human after all.

If you need to get ahead in your career, you should:

- Play to your strengths and use your people skills to get what you want.
- Try not to overthink your career – make a plan and go for it!

Life is too short so don't become stuck in a career you don't love. Stay focused and you will get there. The Loyalist has a lot to offer, so show off your skills and believe! (Enneagram Type 6 - The Loyalist, 2020)[xlv].

Master your finances by honing your skills

The Loyalist is great at managing their budget when you are at healthy levels. Sometimes, your stresses, worries and insecurities can distract you, and bring out the irrational in you. You need to be cautious of this, because we can change our spending habits in line with how we feel and this can mean we lose control of our spending.

You can develop your skills further and learn to master your finances. To do this, you should:

- Make sure that you keep a clear head when making financial decisions.
- Keep tight financial records and monitor all income and expenditure.
- Always only buy things you can afford and don't buy on impulse. Ask yourself three questions – *Do you want the item? Do you need the item? Can you afford it?*
- Be methodical and set clear targets in relation to your finances.

As you are a great thinker, and you do your research, you have strong skills that you could use to master your finances. You should look at securing your money for the future too!

Build emotional, mental, and physical health practices that work best for *The Loyalist*

The Loyalist worries a lot, and worry brings so many stresses and strains. Caring for your emotional, mental and physical health should be top of our to-do list, and yet it always finds its place at the bottom.

Although it isn't as obvious as some, *The Loyalist* can allow anxiety to overwhelm them. They don't always show this on the outside, but things still affect them on the inside. Working on their anxiety issues that stem from worrying is key for your mental and emotional health so it's important to try and stop allowing them to control you. You can do this by:

- Writing down your worries. You can then figure out a strategy to overcome or rationalize it.
- Talk to someone else about your worries and take their opinions on board. *The Loyalist* has an excellent network of support, so use them. What

ever the person advises or suggests is not set in stone, so you can see what others think and still make an informed decision.
- Use aromatherapy to relax. When you are worried, you need to relax and clear your head. Aromatherapy is a great way to do that.

Anxiety can start to take over and this can make us react in an irrational way. Keeping our anxiety under control is key as this stems from worry and stress. One good way to keep your anxiety under control is to work on your inner voice, so you can give yourself a pep talk. To do this, you need to reprogram your mind and ensure you prepare a positive speech to help ease your anxiety. Breathing exercises are another great way to manage anxiety. Breathe out for longer than you breathe in as this gives a calming effect. Try breathing in for 7 seconds and out for 11. This can really help you to stay calm. The only way you're going to permanently solve your anxiety is to get to the bottom of your issue and its triggers. This may be something you can work through yourself with a self-help book, but sometimes, it requires counselling to help you get your thoughts and processes in order, so you can cope better. Remember, getting help is better than suffering, and it's also braver. Make a conscious effort to tackle your anxieties and make the change. You can do it and it'll lift the weight from your shoulders. Often people suffer anxiety and aren't sure why. They really need to dig deep to find out why and this can take time. Give yourself a break – you got this!

For *The Loyalist* it's easy to act on impulse, without thinking things through. This is because you're a reactive person. To avoid acting in an irrational and emotional way, take some steps to control your emotions:

- Don't allow yourself to react immediately.
- Think about the situation and play through what happened in your mind.
- Put yourself in the other person's position – how did they feel?

Physical health is important for *The Loyalist* even though we don't always feel like it. Although you are quite a serious person, there are some exercises to keep you physically fit in a way that suits you:

- Visit the gym. As you're motivated by others, go to the gym. Use a personal trainer or go to the gym with a gym buddy as this will help you to stay motivated.
- Aqua exercises. There are many exercise activities that take place in a swimming pool. Aqua aerobics can be calming, but swimming itself is one of the best exercises you can do.

Looking after your emotional and physical needs are important but you can certainly use the methods that work best for you, to improve. Just remember to seek advice from a qualified medical professional if you suffer from emotional, mental and physical health issues, and you feel that those have escalated.

Become a Leadership Rockstar with your Enneagram skillset

At their best, *The Loyalist* can be a great leader. They are good at forming and strengthening networks, they demand transparency and trust, yet they are caring and defensive of others (this includes their team). *The Loyalist* is all for people, but they also have a creative and innovative streak that inspires others. They live for teamwork, are hard working and very committed.

The Loyalist is protective of their team, and they listen well. Obviously, a team benefits from a leader who has a great level of knowledge and is confident in their own skills, so this is an area that *The Loyalist* can work on. Sixes really need to trust their own problem-solving skills and they are known to be both engaging and responsible which can help them lead effectively.

There's no doubt that sixes make great leaders. In order to transform into a more effective leader, *there are some things they can* improve:

- Trust is a big thing for you, and although you expect it, you don't always give it as easily. You need to work on this and show your team that

you trust them.
- Hold team meetings and set out clear objectives for your team. Use your people skills to bring your team together and create an atmosphere of openness.
- You are the protector of the team, and you should certainly have their back. Don't let this cloud your judgement – allow them to take responsibility for their own actions.
- You can become clingy as you want to hold onto your team, but you need to get the best out of them. Help them achieve their own career dreams and encourage them. A good leader wants their team to do well without worrying about themselves – don't hold them back because they are valuable to you.
- Be open and honest. You worry a lot, so discussing any problems, issues or barriers with your team to get their input is important. You are good at problem solving, but when you worry, you're not at your best. Use your team – you know their skills, qualities and abilities, so involve them and use their knowledge as well as

your own. Sharing ideas is an effective way of working as you get different perspectives. Sharing is caring!

Leadership is perfect for you, but it is possible that your worry and anxiety sets you back. If it helps, you should work on your confidence levels when it comes to being an effective leader. Take on some team leader training or ask to shadow some other team leaders so you can see how they work in comparison to you. This can help you excel in your leadership skills!

Top Tips to Boost your efficiency through problem-solving methods that work for you

For *The Loyalist,* you live for efficiency and you always look for ways to improve. You have already built a team of people that support you and you can utilize them when problem solving. You worry a lot, but it's important that you don't take the weight of the world on your shoulders yourself. If you can contain your worry and keep a clear mind, you can certainly boost your efficiency when problem solving.

To improve their efficiency when it comes to problem-solving, *The Loyalist* should:

- Use your support networks (personal or professional) to help you put your problems into perspective.
- Take part in an activity to calm your mind before you problem solve. You could take a walk, take some time to meditate or you could even take yourself off and read for 30 minutes.
- Use your logical thinking skills, your commitment and your responsible nature to help you to problem solve. Remember to take an objective perspective.
- Follow a problem-solving structure. You could try identifying your problem(s), list your possible solutions and brainstorm them for analysis reasons. Put in place an action plan to help you stay motivated.
- Ensure you show confidence in your solutions – make a list of pros and cons and address them all. Problem-solving isn't easy, so just ensure

you learn from your mistakes and trust your team/friends/family to give you advice – they know you!

Discover a path to spirituality that works best for your personality type

Spirituality works well for *The Loyalist* because they worry a lot and suffer with anxiety. Spirituality can help you to relax and get in touch with your inner voice. Your inner voice is usually negative and fuels your self-doubt. Your spirituality can help you to tap into that negative voice and help you change your mindset.

Spirituality is about clearing your mind and listening to yourself. Of course, spirituality can be a religious term too, but today we'll talk about tapping into ourselves. There are some tips of how *The Loyalist* can be more spiritual, below:

- Create space to allow room for your inner voice. You can meditate, kick back and relax, use breathing exercises or even pray, depending on

your relaxation preference.
- Listen to your inner voice and look for patterns. Write down any negative phrases it says.
- Rationalize what your inner voice tells you and flip it with something positive. Answer back the negative phrase! You can then start to program your inner voice – it must say something positive, before it moves on to being constructive.
- Find your escape – try reading, or walking. Anything that helps you clear your mind and feel good.
- Try a new holistic therapy, like tuning fork therapy. It's a form of sound healing that works on the energy that surrounds you.

The Loyalist often has many insecurities and spirituality can help them deal with this. Having a clear head can make you realize what you really want in life and strive for this. Spirituality can give you a push in the right direction and make you super-efficient.

Connect the dots to create a vision for progress and growth

If your dominant personality is *The Loyalist,* you need to create your growth and progress vision. This is a journey but it's time to maintain healthy levels, shed your anxiety and worry, and develop your ability to trust. To connect the dots and fulfill your vision, we should look at the 9 levels of development for this particular personality type. They will help you to choose your vision for the future, so you can recognize the healthy and unhealthy signs of your personality. You should always strive for healthy levels, 1-3. Average levels are 4-6, but if you find yourself dropping to level 6, you need to really focus on making steady improvements. If your levels are unhealthy (levels 7-9), action is needed now, and you may even need extra support from a medical professional. Remember it's important to monitor your levels.

Healthy levels
Level 1 – This is *The Loyalist* at their very best. They have worked on their trust issues and they are

comfortable and confident when making their own decisions. Even though they work at their best with others, they are independent, positive, and they are effective leaders.

Level 2 – At level 2, *The Loyalist* is appealing, very caring and loving, and they are affectionate. They are able to form strong bonds with others and thrive when they form new networks and long-term relationships. They are happy and feel fulfilled.

Level 3 – At level 3, *The Loyalist* works on building strong relationships with others. They are hard-working, responsible, and most of all, trustworthy. They look to create stability and often sacrifice themselves at work or in their personal life for others. They are dedicated people and demonstrate strong beliefs in things that are important to them. They are excellent at cooperating and encourage others to do this too.

Average levels

Level 4 – At level 4, *The Loyalist* looks for the safe bet. They are organised and look to form alliances that will encourage security. Sixes can be negative at this level, and therefore, they expect problematic situations to occur and remain vigilant in light of this. Most of their time is spent looking for that stability that they crave for in life.

Level 5 – *The Loyalist* can become passive-aggressive when under pressure. They are starting to feel stressed due to the demands made on them and this causes them to react, often without thinking. Sixes start to become indecisive, super-cautious, and they tend to procrastinate a lot. If this behavior escalates, it increases their negativity and anxiety, but they can become confused, unpredictable and can start to be contradictory.

Level 6 – When at level 6, *The Loyalist* often tries to overcompensate for their insecurities. They are in denial at this level and can start to blame others for various events. They use sarcasm and can take a dislike to anyone they feel is not part of their network. They are suspicious and fearful too, and their ability to trust is damaged as they start to see others as threats.

Unhealthy levels

Level 7 – *The Loyalist* is often in panic mode at this level. They feel defensive but long to be stronger. They feel inferior to others and lack self-belief. They berate others and feel very insecure. All of this stress can make sixes react in a volatile way.

Level 8 – At this level, *The Loyalist* takes everything personally. As a result, they react irrationally and even lash out at others. This is because they believe that others are out to get them. Fear gets the better of sixes at this level and it's starting to control aspects of their life.

Level 9 – This is the lowest level and at level 9, *The Loyalist* can become hysterical. They can have developed a paranoid personality disorder, and they are extremely passive-aggressive in nature. They are on the road to self-destruction and can experience suicidal feelings. They want to escape others and often feel like they are being punished.

If you are *The Loyalist* you need to remember that you

have so many skills and qualities, as well as being a genuinely nice person. You have everything you need to excel in your life, but you certainly need to maintain healthy levels to ensure you keep your anxiety in order. When you're in denial, it's difficult to push through the levels, as the first stage to personal growth or improvement is to build your awareness. Just be honest with yourself and others. If you find yourself straying towards the unhealthy levels, you should consider seeking advice from a qualified medical professional. Awareness, acceptance and communication skills are essential for you and your future. (The Enneagram Institute, 2020)[xlvi].

Affirmations for *The Loyalist*

I control my thoughts, feelings, actions and my life.

Others trust and respect me and I treat them in the same way.

I am strong and believe in myself, my decisions and my choices.

Chapter 8

Type Seven: The Enthusiast

Are you spontaneous? Do you get excited over new things? If you answered yes, then maybe *The Enthusiast* is your dominant personality type. *The Enthusiast* is type seven. They love variety and are very flexible. They love to keep busy! Sometimes *The Enthusiast* can be scattered at times and can start to focus on materials things, rather than the things that matter. *The Enthusiast* has many qualities and it's time to start hacking these so you can get the most from your personality type.

Introduction to *The Enthusiast:*

The Enthusiast is a very spirited person that can lighten up your day. They can be playful, yet practical and really appreciate others. Sevens enjoy looking for new, exciting experience but sometimes they stress themselves out as they don't apply their skills and qualities well. This can make them appear disorganized, but they work best when they are focused.

The Enthusiast are positive, and this is a great skill that can take them far. They strive to be content and long for their personal and professional needs to be fulfilled. They have a good sense of humor and often make great leaders because their optimism is infectious.

PROFILE: *The Enthusiast*

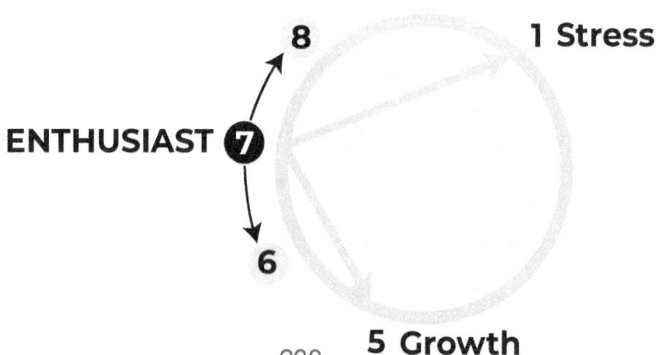

Key Desire: They simply want to feel fulfilled, content and satisfied with life.

Key Fear: Sevens fear pain. They don't want to suffer this, and they also hate to be deprived too.

Wings possibilities: If you find that you are sensitive to the feelings of others, and yet, you are affected by the opinion of others, you could be Enneagram type seven with a six-wing this can make you *The Entertainer.* If you have lots of energy and can be assertive when you need to be, you could have an eight-Wing, which means you are *The Realist.*

Seven with a six-wing: If you have a six-wing, you're *The Entertainer.* That means you are productive and are very optimistic, even when under pressure. You always think on your feet, but sometimes you feel anxious and even doubt your own abilities. This can be a barrier for you, so just be aware of this (Enneagram Type 7w6 - The Pathfinder, 2020)[xlvii].

Seven with an eight-wing: If you have an eight-wing, you are *The Realist.* That means you always stay calm in stressful situations and you are filled with confidence. People are attracted to you because you have charisma, but sometimes you focus too much on your career, and can be impatient and blunt with others. Communicating well with others is something that can enhance your career prospects so keep working on that (Enneagram Type 7w8 - The Opportunist, 2020)[xlviii].

Key motivations: Sevens are motivated by their happiness. Happiness is certainly a key motivator because we all want what makes us happy. They also try to ensure they don't miss out on valuable events or experiences. Freedom also motivates them, and they can use the things they want in life to get them excited. This ensures they keep aiming high.

Strengths: *The Enthusiast,* is enthusiastic to say the least, when they are at healthy levels. They are bold and anticipate all things good. A strong and positive attitude makes them a great leader and portrays them as a natural, authoritative figure. Their nature is cheerful, which means they are engaging, and their spontaneity means they exhilarate others because they are EXCITING. They are great at synthesizing and making sense of ideas, and they are great when it comes to creativity. They have the inner-qualities and skills that they can use to become a huge success. They have great minds and others find this refreshing and attractive.

Stress points and Growth:

As they move into the path of disintegration (stress) towards number 1, they can be over critical and are in danger of becoming a perfectionist. Following the arrow of integration (growth) towards number 5, a type Seven can become focused by life – this way it's easier to keep aiming for what they want (The Enneagram Institute, 2020)[xlix].

How *The Enthusiast* can hack their own success?

You have all the skills for success already, so all you have to do is tap into them. Sevens are responsive, good, eager and cheerful. They work hard and are generally well accomplished. They are multi-talented and are always appreciative of others. These skills enhance their chances of success. To hack their success, they should:

- Don't act on impulse. Make sure you give yourself time to think before you act.
- Your cheery nature is great and it's often infectious, but just ensure you are aware that this can sometimes overwhelm or make others feel uncomfortable. Sometimes, it's necessary to tone this down a little, so be aware of your surroundings and ensure you remain appropriate – especially in a professional capacity.
- Write down how you act/feel/think and use lists to gain your perspective. Whenever you find yourself reacting irrationally, note down the pros and cons, brainstorm ideas, write down how you wanted to react and how you reacted, think about your triggers – *what makes you act irrationally?*
- As you are an energetic person, you burn a lot of energy. Ensure you keep yourself well hydrated and have plenty of healthy snacks at your disposal. People with high-energy need to constantly refuel.

Goal setting is the key to success but at first you need to figure out what you want. Take a few moments to contemplate what success means to you. Then set yourself some baby steps to get there. Once you have this, you have the basis for a plan and it's something for you to work towards.

The Enthusiast can become anxious and this makes them demanding and pushy when they feel these pressures. Make sure you take care of yourself and get enough rest. Ensure you deal with any anxieties you feel too, as this can sometimes trigger your impulsivity.

You are a naturally positive person, so use it and believe in your own success. This could certainly be the key for you!

Using the enneagram to achieve self-improvement

Don't be precious – we can all improve ourselves. We learn and absorb information everyday. We've talked about sevens being impulsive and they often make decisions or take action, immediately because they have a sense of impatience. We can develop our skills and qualities for self-improvement purposes.

If you're *The Enthusiast* and you want to improve yourself, you should focus on what provokes a reaction from you:

- Keep a journal that details every time you act or feel like acting on impulse. *Write down what you did – what was the impulsive act? How would you like to react?*
- Learn to be patient. You need to control the tantrum in yourself as you often react to certain situations.
- Create a wall of inspiration. Take one wall in your home and fill it with things that inspire you. Pictures, vision boards, brainstorms, affirmations, color and anything else you're proud of. This could be something like a certificate of a course you've recently completed. This will keep you motivated!

The Enthusiast has many skills and qualities, but they

can still improve themselves. For further self-improvement, *The Enthusiast* needs to maintain their energy levels and learn to control how they react and ensure they don't react without thinking.,

Strengthening Relationships – tapping into your own strengths

Sevens have a lot of positive traits to bring to professional, family and romantic relationships. They are optimistic, enthusiastic, and they are great at adapting. They can sometimes have trouble committing and settling down, and they have trouble facing serious or negative conversations, as they are not always comfortable with such emotions. They are not always great listeners, but they are very encouraging and often encourage others to try new things.

The Enthusiast is often a fun person to be around. They have lots of energy and can motivate others if they need a push. They do need to consider others in their life too, because sometimes their impulsive decisions impact others and there can be consequences. A relationship is two-sided so it's important to work together, but this isn't something that *The Enthusiast* finds easy.

Sevens can get bored easily, but they have creative ideas and like others to appreciate these. Sometimes their commitment issues prevent them from finishing things, and this can be frustrating others. This is something we can work on.

If a seven is surrounded by negativity, it can result in them feeling anxious as they start to feel stressed. A seven longs for freedom, which can also hinder their relationships. It's important that a seven considers the needs of the people they have a relationship with, but also that they are honest about their needs in a relationship too. Let people know you – tell them you need freedom, positivity and that you get bored easily.

Now, if sevens want to strengthen their relationships, there are some things they can do:

- Face your commitment issues and talk this through with the person you are in a relationship

with. Honestly is the best policy!
- Learn to listen to others. Take some time to listen to others and digest what they are saying.
- Write a list of the negative situations or conversations you usually avoid and think about how you can handle them in a more positive way. We have to learn to cope and deal with situations effectively before anxiety kicks in.

To strengthen relationships, a seven needs to work really hard on their listening skills. It's easy to become overwhelmed by the negative things that happen, or the things that don't interest us, but you need to move away from that mindset, and adopt a new one. You're not alone when you're in a relationship, so you need to consider the feelings and needs of the other person too. *The Enthusiast* has so many qualities to bring to a relationship.

Sevens are great people and their positivity is refreshing. They are fun and exciting, so take all of those traits into your relationship and boss it! (Relationship Type 7 with Type 7 — The Enneagram

Institute, 2020)[i].

Achieving your career potential

There are many career opportunities for *The Enthusiast.* You are creative thinkers and you have a great imagination. You have high energy levels and are constantly exploring new ideas which makes you great at motivating others. You would be great in careers that involved project work, leading or mentoring, or were linked to creative or expressive arts. You are social and always have something to offer, so others are excited to have you as part of their team. You never want to stagnate and constantly aim to drive forward.

A seven works best with others. They love exploring new ideas and experiencing new things. Great careers for sevens include designing roles, writing roles, photography, publicity or marketing roles, and roles in travel or entertainment would be great for you because of your energy. As a people person, you're an effective team player, but you need to ensure you are utilizing your listening skills too.

If you want to achieve your career potential, you need to ensure you:

- Keep yourself busy. You know you work best when you don't feel bored so use your creativity.
- Keep using your optimism to motivate others. Use your social skills to get to know your team and make use of your positive, creative nature.
- Perhaps take on some online courses or read self-help books. Start to apply them to the workplace.
- Work on being more organized. Sure, you don't like rules and schedules, but they will help you to progress in your career. This is certainly something you can work on. Write yourself to-do lists and goals to help you with those organization skills.

To succeed in your career, think about what you want in the long term. Everyone has to work hard for their career, so don't underestimate what you need to do:

- Make a personal development plant to get you

to your preferred or chosen career.

- Make sure you set plenty of objectives and targets so that you remain interested and enthusiastic. Keep challenging yourself so you don't get bored.

You want a career that excites you. Something you can feel excited about (Enneagram Type 7 - The Adventurer, 2020) [li].

Master your finances by honing your skills

As *The Enthusiast* is resilient, logical and positive at their best, they have some excellent skills when honing their finances. It's in everyone's best interests to maximize their finances. You can develop the skills you already have in order to master your finances:

- Make sure you log and analyze your finances effectively. Make a spreadsheet or note down your money in your notebook. Account for every penny and log into your bank account everyday to check your balance.

- Use your problem-solving skills to discover if the spends are worthwhile.
- You can be impulsive, so you need to slow down when it comes to spending money. Carefully evaluate if you can afford the item and whether you just want the item or need it.
- Be honest and don't be afraid to get advice from others regarding your finances if you need it. Sometimes a fresh pair of eyes or professional advice is needed.

When you're at healthy levels, you are modest and reasonable when it comes to your finances, but *The Enthusiast* is known to be unpredictable and impulsive. You need to be careful that you don't carry that into your finances. You are a practical and creative thinker, and you can use this to maximize your finances. Keep a level head when reviewing your finances.

Build emotional, mental, and physical health practices that work best for *The Enthusiast*

The Enthusiast can suffer with serious FOMO (fear of

missing out). They don't like feeling deprived and they fear pain, but fear can take over our lives as it causes worry, stress and anxiety. With these fears leading to so many underlying issues, it's important that sevens take care of their own emotional, mental and physical health. In this section, we're going to look at some of the health practices that will work best for you.

It's important that you don't let your emotional and mental health close you off to the world and prevent you from listening. Here are some ideas to help you build emotional and mental health practices:

- Don't ignore your worries and feelings. Note them down and their causes in a notebook or journal. Find out what makes you tick, and what makes you happy.
- You love being around a wide range of people, so think about the people you are close to. Talk to them and ask for their opinions.
- Color Therapy would be great for *The Enthusiast* and it's something that you might really enjoy. Book yourself some sessions!

- Taking care of your body can really help your emotional and mental health, so why not take a massage too.

Don't beat yourself up if you feel or react in a negative way. We can all react in a negative way from time to time, and this is often due to a stressful event or worry, that has started to cause anxiety. You have high-energy, but sometimes this results in a dip of exhaustion. We can help our own mental and emotional health by reacting in a different way. You are in control of your own actions and emotions, so with that in mind:

- Count to thirty in your head and take a couple of deep breaths while you're doing this before you react to a situation.
- Consider the pros and cons. Play through the worst and best outcome in your mind.
- Be objective. Separate yourself from situation or put yourself in the shoes of another. Think about what they did and how they felt.

It's well known that exercise can help our mental health

as well as our physical so you should certainly try and exercise daily. Something simple like a walk or skipping can make a difference to your daily routine and increase your heart rate. You should certainly look at doing at least 30 minutes of exercise each day.

It's important that we look after ourselves, and as you have a lot of energy exercise is something that you will. You are quite a motivated person, but it's still important to remember that emotional, mental and physical health is important. Although it's probably difficult for you, you still need to find time to relax. The therapy sessions like a massage or color therapy mentioned earlier in this section will be invaluable for you.

Become a Leadership Rockstar with your Enneagram skillset

The Enthusiast has all the tools to become a great leader. They build a network of people because they are an extrovert, and others find their energy and spontaneity attractive and motivating.

As sevens find life a great adventure, they can be effective when leading a team. They are creative and bold, but most of all they are cheerful. They are great thinkers and they find their ideas and the ideas of others exhilarating. They love being part of different initiatives and they are great at brainstorming and problem solving.

Sevens make great leaders, but they can become more effective leaders; *there are some things they can improve:*

- You have a range of skills, so you can be an effective leader by training your team on a regular basis.
- All great leaders should hold team meetings and set clear objectives and goals as a whole team. Allow others to take ownership.
- Ensure that you work on your own fears, worries and anxieties, as they can hinder you and your team. You should be open and honest, but you are great at solving problems, so discuss any barriers that are relevant to the team but keep

an open mind.
- Lead by example. Your energy and positivity inspire others so keep it up and use it to motivate and encourage your team.
- You can develop your leadership skills by listening to your team and ensuring they feel like they can talk to you. This will help them feel valued and respected. If you treat your team well, they will often be more productive. Keep developing yourself and your team, and you will thrive as a leader!

Top Tips to Boost your efficiency through problem-solving methods that work for you

Your problem-solving skills are already outstanding. You have a positive response to most things because you are grateful and appreciative of everything that happens in your life.

To improve their efficiency when it comes to problem-solving, *The Enthusiast* should:

- Listen to others and ask for the opinions or advice from others when you need to identify or solve a problem.
- Use your logical thinking skills, your commitment and your responsible nature to help you to problem solve. Remember to take an objective perspective.
- Everybody needs to use a structured problem-solving approach, and as you have a creative mind and lots of energy, you can contribute or even lead this well. You should first identify your problem(s), list your possible solutions and brainstorm them for analysis reasons. Put in place an action plan to help you stay motivated.
- If there are aspects that worry you about the problem, talk through them with others. Sure, sometimes you're a 'suffer in silence' type, but you'll be much more productive if you talk things through.

Discover a path to spirituality that works best for your personality type

You have so much energy to burn, but when do you really find time to relax? Spirituality can really help you with this and it can also help you recognize how you can be appreciative of yourself and others. Sometimes, you can be acquisitive, and this means you lose sight of things. You also don't always listen to others and sometimes you overlook what they are suggesting. This isn't intentional, but because you are eager and like to get things done fast. Spirituality can increase your mindfulness.

Mindfulness is when you are fully aware and attentive to everything that is happening around you. This can increase our spirituality as it brings a sense of awareness about ourselves and ensures we are in-tune you're your body and mind. It helps us to identify when we are anxious, stressed or overwhelmed, but it can also help us to identify things in relation to our own actions, and we react negatively. Mindfulness can also include meditation which can also help us get in touch with our spiritual side. There are some tips of how *The Enthusiast* can be more mindful, below:

- Slow down and put your phone away. Life can be so busy, and we can be distracted by our phones. Take some time to slow down and turn off your phone and social media. Take the time to relax and reflect.
- Practice listening. Make a conscious effort to listen to others when they are speaking and give them your full attention. Listen actively!
- Ask yourself how you are feeling. Kick back for five minutes every night and notice how you're feeling. Ask yourself, *how am I? How was my day?* Really consider what made you happy and what didn't. Think about those things that made you anxious or what made you light up. Think about the why – *why do you feel this way?* This is a great way to figure out what you need in life and then you can ensure you keep striving for a happier life.
- When you wake up, do some breathing and stretching. Light exercise can really help you to

refocus your mind.
- Do something creative. Draw, paint, write, read, bake, for instance, or anything else that makes you happy. Some people enjoy coloring books, and you can get adult books too. They can help people relax too.
- Allow yourself to think about the future. Visualize it and dream about the future. Think about it every day and think about how you're going to get there, and how close you are to getting there. Ensure you've got goals so you can measure your progress.
* Practice gratitude. Everyday think about those things you're thankful for and be grateful for them.

The Enthusiast will certainly benefit from spirituality. It can help you to heal your soul and if you consider your positive nature, it can help you grow! Spirituality can really push you in the right direction, and you think more clearly when you can clear your mind. You can also be more attentive to the needs of others as well as yourself.

Connect the dots to create a vision for progress and growth

If your dominant personality is *The Enthusiast,* then you can start to create your vision for growth and progress. To connect the dots, we need to look at the 9 levels of development for this particular personality type. They will help you to choose your vision for the future, so you can recognize the healthy and unhealthy signs of your personality. You should always strive for healthy levels, 1-3. Average levels are 4-6, but if you find yourself dropping to level 6, you need to really focus on making steady improvements. If your levels are unhealthy (levels 7-9), action is needed now, and you may even need extra support from a medical professional. Remember it's important to monitor your levels.

Healthy levels
Level 1 – This is *The Enthusiast* at their very best and they are filled with goodness. They are so grateful for everything they have in life. They are appreciative of others, kind, and generous. They are quite spiritual, which makes them very joyous. They incorporate their

experiences in life and learn from them. They love to help others and are generally happy and fulfilled with life.

Level 2 – At level 2, *The Enthusiast* is very lively and vivacious. They are an extrovert and are therefore confident around people. They are highly responsive and look forward to new experiences. It drives them and makes them excitable. They are resilient in nature and are eager to learn new things.

Level 3 – At level 3, *The Enthusiast* is often very productive. They can become high achievers as they are multi-talented. They are very practical people and they are very determined in life. They are very energetic and live to do a variety of different things. They love to be spontaneous too!

Average levels
Level 4 – At level 4, *The Enthusiast* wants more options and choices in life. They are adventurous and less focused, but they are very wise to the world. They love to try new things and they enjoy keeping up with the

latest trends because they love to consume. Money is important to you, and you are quite sophisticated.

Level 5 – *The Enthusiast* at this stage can be hyperactive. They say whatever comes into their mind and they can start to exaggerate. They are witty in nature, but they like to stay busy as they don't like to be bored. The issue is that they often take on too much. They have so many ideas – probably too many. They like to throw themselves into sometime and when they do, they are fully committed, but they need to get used to saying 'no' once in a while.

Level 6 – When at level 6, *The Enthusiast* is often unsatisfied, insensitive and hardened. They can be quite selfish and only think about the things that they want. The material things! They can start to be very demanding and sometimes a little flamboyant too. Their anxieties can start to show their ugly head too which can be overwhelming for them.

Unhealthy levels
Level 7 – *The Enthusiast* can start to be offensive at

this stage. They are quite anxious, but they can be child-like as once they start being negative, they don't know how to stop. They are desperate to soothe their anxieties and like to escape from the big bad world they live in. They can also be impulsive, with an addictive nature. They can start to lose control and become abusive towards others.

Level 8 – At this level, *The Enthusiast* often has erratic mood swings. They are out of control, compulsive and they act on impulse. They are dealing with a lot of anxiety at this stage that they need to resolve, but rather than dealing with it, they act irrationally. They act out regularly and become frustrated easily.

Level 9 – This is the lowest level and at level 9, *The Enthusiast* is suffering. They have very little energy and their health is deteriorating. They are exhausted and can feel lethargic and suffer with a type of personality disorder like Bipolar. They have given up and feel depressed. Their level of despair is at a critical level and they are in the depths of despair. They feel panicky, and sometimes indulge in suicidal behavior.

If you are *The Enthusiast,* you must understand the importance of maintaining healthy levels. They can be a great leader and are great at motivating others, but they need to be more in-tune with their own needs and the needs of others. You are destined for great things, so keep going! (The Enneagram Institute, 2020)[lii]

Affirmations for *The Enthusiast*

Wonderful things will happen to me and I deserve it.

I trust my intuition and wisdom. I allow them to guide me to make the right decision.

I never give up if I don't succeed, but I know I will achieve my dreams if I keep trying.

Chapter 9

Type Eight: The Challenger

Do you find that sometimes you take the lead or take over? Are you the driving force? Maybe you're powerful? If this is the case, you could be Enneagram personality type eight, *The Challenger.* They are self-confident people who are easily assertive and decisive. They are often resourceful too, but their personality can be quite controlling and confrontational at times. Overall, you are very inspiring, and your strength is your ability to improve yourself and others.

Introduction to *The Challenger:*

The Challenger is very courageous, and they MUST achieve their visions and goals, even if it significantly impacts them. They are great people and at their best, they are self-restrained, merciful and able to master their own abilities. Their confidence is an attractive trait because of their positive attitude and drive. They are seen as inspirational leaders as leading comes naturally to them. This is because you are a champion! Your intentions are always honorable, and you show initiative and strength in everything you do. *The Challenger* is in danger of becoming too domineering. Sometimes their ego makes them quite confrontational and intimidating and that's because they don't like to be called out on anything or feel like they are being criticized. In order to be successful, you need to get over this. It's fine to be resourceful and straight-talking, but ensure you show empathy and compassion too as this is you at your best.

PROFILE: *The Challenger*

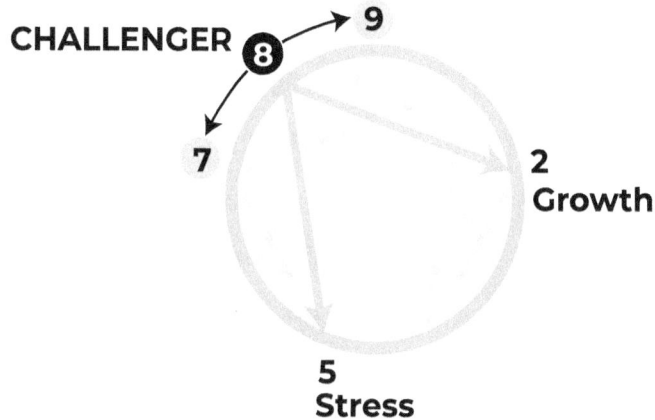

Key Desire: The Challenger wants to be in control of their own life. They simply want to protect themselves.

Key Fear: The Challenger does not like to feel as if others are trying to control or harm them. This is their biggest fear.

Wings possibilities: If you're a natural leader, and like to form connections with others you may have a seven-wing and that means you are *The Maverick*. If you're supportive and protective of those you care about, then you could have nine-wing, and this would mean you are *The Bear*.

Eight with a seven-wing: If you have a

seven-wing, you're *The Maverick.* They are generally very optimistic, and others find them inspirational. They are open when it comes to their thoughts and opinions, and this allows them to form strong bonds with others. Sometimes, you have difficulty listening to authority figures, and you can sometimes be insensitive when dealing with others. This is something you can grow and develop (Enneagram Type 8w7 - The Nonconformist, 2020)[liii].

Eight with a nine-wing: If you have a nine-wing, you're *The Bear.* You are naturally energetic, and you are very confident. You lead well, and you are good at being attentive to others. You can be stubborn and struggle to control your temper, but this is something that you can work to overcome (Enneagram Type 8w9 - The Diplomat, 2020)[liv].

Key motivations: Eights are constantly trying to prove themselves as they love to be important and make an impact. They can sometimes try to control everything. They love to show how independent they are.

Strengths: *The Challenger,* is confident and

courageous at their best. They have mastered their higher authority and will do anything to achieve their goals. They are driven and constantly strive to achieve their goals. They are powerful leaders and very strong and assertive too. They are an inspiration to others, resourceful, and they are great at motivating and improving others.

Stress points and Growth:

As they move into the path of disintegration (stress) towards number 5, they can start to become fearful and also secretive. Following the arrow of integration (growth) towards number 2, Type Eights are often healthy, happy, kind and caring (The Enneagram Institute, 2020)[iv].

How *The Challenger* can hack their own success?

You are already courageous and strong, with the tools to keep striving for your own success. If you keep going on the right path and maintain your healthy levels, then you can easily hack your own success. But there are some things you can do to ensure you don't start dipping into those unhealthy levels. If you are committed to your own success, then you should:

- Be careful not to confuse control with drive and determination. Others rely on you to drive them forward, but make sure you don't take over.
- You often inspire others, so use this and inspire yourself.
- Monitor your own behavior, actions, emotions and thought patterns by writing them down. *Did you react in the way you should? If not, how should you have reacted?*
- Although you like to stand alone, work on your social and team working skills. Build on these skills because these skills can help you to be successful in your career.

Everyone should set goals regardless of their personality type. Goals help us to stay focused and head for what we really want. All you need to do, is decide what that is. *What does success mean to you?* You can then start thinking about how you can achieve it. *What do you need to do to be successful?*

You are a natural leader, but you are in danger of becoming too dominating and this intimidates others. Use your initiative, as that 'can-do' attitude of yours is appealing and attracts others. It can certainly contribute to your success.

Using the enneagram to achieve self-improvement

You regularly try to improve yourself – it's in your nature. There are many things you're already good at but it would naïve to think that there's nothing to improve – we can all improve at something. There are some things that you don't see as 'needing' improvement and this is sometimes where eights go wrong and start to sift into those unhealthy levels. You often distance yourself from others and you fear being rejected, but this can damage your ability to self-improve. You need to ensure you don't shut down and block the people you have a connection to. When it comes to your ego, you're sensitive, and yet you tell others that they shouldn't be sensitive. It's time to talk about how you can improve and keep those things in check.

If you're *The Challenger* you should:

- Work on your fears of being hurt and rejected. Fears holds us back, so we need to control it. There are some things beyond our control that we have to accept, but we can control how we handle our fear by facing it.
- Write a list of things you want to improve about yourself. Look at each of these things and give a reason why you want to improve that particular thing. Then prioritize them – put them in order of importance. You can then work on making those improvements.
- Increase your social interactions and work on your team working skills. Sometimes, you block others, but you need to monitor this. Ensure you show yourself and others the respect they deserve.

The Challenger is persistent and strong, and they often look for this strength in others too. They have excellent willpower and therefore, they often succeed when trying to develop themselves. Just maintain healthy levels and ensure you don't overlook your health and wellbeing.

Strengthening Relationships – tapping into your own strengths

When it comes to relationships, eights, like to be the more dominant person. Their willpower is strong and are very independent. This can sometimes be difficult as they are used to being the decision-maker which can sometimes mean there isn't an equal balance in their personal and professional relationships.

The Challenger has lots of energy and vitality, and this is a great trait as it makes them a great person to be around. It takes an eight a while to trust someone, but when they do, they are protective of them. They are relieved when they find a dependable person that they can have confidence in.

An eight doesn't always find it easy to work as a team, but this is something that they get used to in a relationship. They can also be suspicious, reactive, confrontational and volatile when things aren't going their way. If you want to strengthen your relationships, it's best to work on these conflicts and learn how to control your feelings and emotions to a certain degree, or even process your feelings differently.

Above all, you are very loyal and others love this about you. You have a generous and happy nature, but don't forget to apologize and admit fault when appropriate. Sometimes, your sensitive nature makes you vulnerable and you don't like that. Take some space on your own to think, as often, when you process the situation again in your mind, and you get over the initial anger, you'll find you've overreacted or could've at least answered better.

Now, if eights want to strengthen their relationships, there are some things they can do:

- Talk to others. Don't be afraid to express your concerns and work on those trust issues.
- Ensure your behavior and aggression is under control. You can do this by working on how you process your thoughts, feelings and actions.

Maybe cognitive behavioral therapy will help!
- Work on your ego. Your ego stops you from doing things and it's why you want to be right, and dominate every situation.

To strengthen relationships, an eight needs to ensure they don't overreact when it comes to trivial situations and must work to sort out differences. Although they are strong in character, it's time to accept that they are not always right. Being right isn't important, but honesty, integrity and energy is, and you have all three of those traits. They are excellent qualities to bring to your relationships and will only strengthen them, and ensure they are long-lasting (Relationship Type 8 with Type 8 — The Enneagram Institute, 2020)[lvi].

Achieving your career potential

You are known as being *The Challenger* because you challenge yourself and others and bring out the best in others, turning them into the best they can be. This is a fantastic skill of yours. You love to lead and strive on performance and success. There's part of you that works to protect others too, and you have strong values that lead you through life.

An eight works best when they are in charge, so that they can set goals and lead the way. They make great teachers, principals, and directors, but as they want truth and justice in life, they also work well in a legal field, as a lawyer, a judge, or possibly law enforcement. They have great planning skills and are great at leading challenging projects. Their career prospects expand further over time as eights are natural managers, leaders, and business owners. They have strategic thinking abilities and can motivate others into taking action.

If you want to achieve your career potential, some important things you should note:

- Grow your leadership and management skills for the future by working on your ability to listen and take responsibility for yourself and your team. This means admitting when you are wrong which isn't easy for an eight.

- You are an inspiration. Keep inspiring people by using your creative and strategic thinking skills.
- *Have you worked on your ego yet?* If not, you have to. This will ensure you lead by example and keep heading for improvements.
- Finally, keep challenging yourself and others and ensure you do this in a professional way. Set goals, push yourself and your colleagues/team, and strive to be a better person.

To succeed in your career, think about the direction you want to head in.

- Create your career plan and add a personal development section. This way you can plan any skills, experience, training or qualifications you need to achieve your chosen career. This will give you something to aim for.
- Think about emotional health when you're striving for your career. It's important for eights to stay emotionally healthy, so that they can manage their need for being in control and any feelings of frustration.

Choose a career that you love and enjoy. Although you like a challenge, you don't like stress, and a career that you enjoy relieves that pressure (Enneagram Type 8 - The Protector, 2020)[lvii].

Master your finances by honing your skills

The Challenger likes to control as much as they possibly can, and that includes their finances. You are already good at this, but you can develop further and master your finances:

- Keep track of your finances and log everything that comes in and out down to the penny. This will help you to account for everything.
- Build a financial plan. There's no reason to suggest that you're not good with money. You should really make the most of this by having a financial plan. You might find an investment opportunity – maybe invest in yourself. You could also consider a savings or growth plan for your money too.
- Be realistic with your money. Don't tie too much

up in other things as everyone needs access for cashflow purposes. If you aren't realistic, it could lead to financial hardship. Be logical and ensure you really assess your financial situation, for example, don't invest more than you can afford.
- Although you like to stay in control, don't be afraid to get advice from a financial expert if you need further advice or guidance.

The Challenger loves to be in control and is not particularly materialistic. The bulk of money you spend is on bettering yourself and your prospects but sometimes this puts too much pressure on you. Don't make rash decisions, and ensure you assess your financial options objectively. We know you are a sensible person, so get help when making important financial decisions too. It's in your nature to look for challenges when it comes to learning or earning more money, and these are also strengths of yours. You have the ability to master and make the most of your finances, so don't waste your opportunities!

Build emotional, mental, and physical health practices that work best for *The Challenger*

You constantly want more and strive for improvements, and this can be draining. *The Challenger* is known for taking on too much and sometimes this can affect our emotional, mental and physical health practices. You can become really frustrated, which can lead to anger. That's why it's important to keep your health in check, as to avoid you overloading and becoming volatile.

First of all, let's talk about physical health. Exercise is great for you because you have lots of energy. If you do feel frustrated, exercise is great to stimulate your mind and work up any anger or stress you've built up inside. Great exercises for you would be:

- Skipping. Skipping is a great cardio exercise and you can do this in the comfort of your own home or even in your yard.
- Boxing or boxing-themed aerobics. This is a great exercise regime that gets you moving, and the boxing movements are great for burning fat,

energy and any pent-up frustrations you feel.
- Walking. Walking is a great way to exercise as it gets you thinking. You can change the difficulty to suit you by walking slow, fast, or even powerwalking. You can also step it up further by using intermittent jogging. This is when you walk for 1 minute, jog for the next minute, then repeat.

Your emotional and mental health is important too. You must take care of this to help you remain positive. It also helps you to clear you mind so that you can start listening and remove any blocks that prevent your communication:

- Take some time for self-discovery. Get in touch with your inner-self and your inner-voice. Some people find journaling useful, so note down your thoughts, feelings and actions, and think about the things that made you happy, sad, frustrated etc… This will help to build your self-awareness.
- When you feel frustrated about something, talk about it. Ensure there is someone you can talk to. This should be a friend, a family member, or

there are even hotlines you can call to talk through your worries. These people are trained to deal with these types of things.
- Breathing techniques are great calming techniques. You can then self-reflect and assess situations before you act.
- Use yoga and meditation to clear your mind and ensure you can relax and think clearly.
- Holistic therapies such as a massage would also benefit you, as it can be a great stress-reliever.

You should spend time each day working on your physical, emotional and mental health. We all need to look after ourselves, as we need to refuel our energy in order to keep going. You have lots of energy but it's important to try to relax. Try reading – it can be great to escape in a good book!

Become a Leadership Rockstar with your Enneagram skillset

The Challenger has great leadership skills as we've already discussed. They love a challenge, naturally take over, have creative and inspirational ideas, and they have a powerful nature.

Eights can be assertive, confident and very resourceful as leaders. They know what they want, and they are great at planning projects and increasing performance. Another excellent leadership quality is the fact that they are protective of their team and they live to help others improve. All of these qualities mean that they are effective leaders.

Eights can become even better leaders if they:

- Work on their listening skills and listen to their team.
- Develop their teamworking skills.
- Control their frustrations and refrain from being confrontational. It's important to be professional when in a role of authority.
- You inspire others and have great thinking abilities. Use them to drive and motivate your team.
- Give recognition and lose your ego – take

responsibility, be accountable and problem solve, rather than becoming frustrated when things don't go your way.

You have the makings of a great leader when you maintain your healthy levels. Your career will flourish if you continue to grow and self-improve.

Top Tips to Boost your efficiency through problem-solving methods that work for you

You're a strategic thinker, and therefore, you are able to problem-solve in a logical and formulaic way. Your resourcefulness precedes you and you always search for answers, but this can sometimes be intimidating, which makes other people close-down. If you can't find the answer you become frustrated and when you're frustrated, you're in danger of not listening to others as your communication skills start to close down. Take a breath and use your willfulness and logic to find creative ways around any barriers.

To improve their efficiency when it comes to

problem-solving, *The Challenger* should:

- Maintain professionalism. Ensure that they aren't aggressive with others who are problem-solving with them or trying to help.
- Make sure they take the opinions and thoughts of others into account by listening to their ideas.
- Open communication channels by being approachable and encouraging others to share their ideas.
- Lead the problem-solving process, and keep people focused on identifying the problem and solution. Sometimes this means using a problem-solving formula. If you hold a meeting when problem solving, you need to facilitate an agreement amongst the attendees such that there's no such thing as a bad idea/question and set a rule that everyone must contribute to the discussion. This will ensure you get maximum impact from your meeting.

Discover a path to spirituality that works best for your personality type

As an energetic person, spirituality isn't something you always strive for. Finding ways to relax, becoming self-aware and getting in touch with our inner voice can help us to generally become a calmer person. You can also use CBT techniques (Cognitive Behavioral Therapy), Mindfulness and Rapid Transformational Therapy (RTT) too. RTT is what we will focus on as a way to get in touch with your inner-self and to help you overcome the personal setbacks in your life.

For *The Challenger,* everything is busy and you don't always give yourself time to process your own thoughts and feelings. When you suffer a setback, it makes you feel frustrated and sometimes even angry. You then don't deal with this, and it causes further problems. With RTT you can see speedy results. If you don't know what RTT is, you should explore this further, but in a nutshell, it's a way to reprogram your subconscious mind and it embraces hypnotherapy techniques. If you don't know what RRT is exactly or you've never heard of it before, you can watch video clips and even engage in sessions on Youtube or alternatively, you can get yourself a therapist that specialists in RTT.:

You're probably thinking, *why RTT?* The answer is simple... RTT has many, many benefits that can really help *The Challenger* and improve how they can transform in a spiritual way. The benefits of RTT include:

- It can help you clarify, refine and pursue your life goals.
- It can help you heal from past experiences and even trauma.
- It's helpful when dealing and healing from abuse. This could be mental, sexual, or physical.
- You can reprogram your unhealthy eating habits and it can even help you maintain a normal weight.
- It can boost your confidence.
- It can improve your ability to fight against depression, stress, insomnia and anxiety.
- Your communication skills will improve.

- It's useful if you want to quit additions like smoking, drinking, food or sex.

The Challenger will certainly benefit from spirituality. This could come in the form of RTT, mindfulness or self-awareness based on CBT. All of these things can help you to heal and grow as a person. It will help you to get everything you want in life.

Connect the dots to create a vision for progress and growth

If your dominant personality is *The Challenger,* it's time to create your vision. To connect the dots, we need to look at the 9 levels of development for this particular personality type. They will help you to choose your vision for the future, so you can recognize the healthy and unhealthy signs of your personality. You should always strive for healthy levels, 1-3. Average levels are 4-6, but if you find yourself dropping to level 6, you need to really focus on making steady improvements. If your levels are unhealthy (levels 7-9), action is needed now, and you may even need extra support from a medical professional. Remember it's important to monitor your levels.

Healthy levels

Level 1 – This is *The Challenger* at their very best and they are very courageous and willful. Sometimes they sacrifice themselves to achieve their vision. They long to give an impression so that they are remembered for their greatness. They are self-restrained, and they have mastered their higher authority. They are very merciful and considerate, as well as being patient.

Level 2 – At level 2, *The Challenger* is resourceful and has a positive attitude towards everything. They are passionate, driven and filled with confidence. They know how to get what they want in life. They are strong, assertive and they are not afraid to stand up for what they believe in.

Level 3 – At level 3, *The Challenger* is a protector of others. They are authentic and use their strength to help others succeed. They are great at making decisions and they lead well. Others often look up to them because they have initiative, and they are great at motivating others.

Average levels

Level 4 – At level 4, *The Challenger* is financially independent and pragmatic. They work hard, and although they take risks, they are self-sufficient. Sometimes at this level, the challenger starts to deny their own emotional needs, and this can affect their ability to communicate.

Level 5 – *The Challenger* tries to dominate everything. They are proud, but they are very willful and strive only for their vision. They can become forceful and often boast about their own achievements. At this stage, they can stop treating others as equals and can show lack of respect. Yet, they like to feel that they are supported by others and this can affect their relationships.

Level 6 – When at level 6, *The Challenger* can be quite intimidating and unapproachable. They cause conflict by being confrontational and they will not back down. They are very insecure and can treat others unfairly.

This causes resentment as they often threaten others to get support from others.

Unhealthy levels

Level 7 – *The Challenger* can feel like the world is against them. They defy any attempt at help, because they feel that others are trying to control them. They are ruthless and they lose their sense of morals. They can become aggressive and volatile too.

Level 8 – At this level, *The Challenger* has delusional ideas and sees themselves as being powerful. They believe that they are invincible and that nothing can stop them. They are reckless, yet still believe they will achieve. They start to spiral out of control and cannot see any wrong in their behavior.

Level 9 – This is the lowest level and at level 9, *The Challenger* is in danger at this stage. They have sociopathic tendencies and display signs of antisocial personality disorders. If something or someone does not conform to their ideas, they become vengeful. They seek to destroy everything and anyone, rather than change their own ways or beliefs. They must seek urgent help, but they don't see the destructive nature of their behavior.

If you are *The Challenger,* you must understand the importance of maintaining healthy levels as the unhealthy levels for you are dangerous. You are confident and driven, but there are some vital things you can work from. You would make a great leader and will keep being promoted at work because of your need to achieve! (The Enneagram Institute, 2020)[lviii]

Affirmations for *The Challenger*

I don't worry about things beyond my control and accept that I can't control everything.

I am worthy of success and offer my gratitude to those who have helped me.

I appreciate others. I care for the people in my life. I inspire them and I'm always there to listen and help.

Chapter 10

Type Nine: The Peacemaker

Are you always looking for the peaceful solution? Maybe you're the easy going one? Will you do anything for peace? If so, you could be Enneagram personality type 9, *The Peacemaker*. They are receptive, easygoing, and optimistic. They trust others implicitly and are supportive of others. *The Peacemaker* has a way of simplifying problems and they are very kind.

Introduction to *The Peacemaker:*

The Peacemaker is typically creative and optimistic. They like to look on the bright side and are very supportive. You can always rely on them as they embrace their family and friends. They are trustworthy and always try to resolve conflict by smoothing things over. They can sometimes be stubborn, but on the whole, they want a peaceful life and often bring people together.

PROFILE: *The Peacemaker*

Key Desire: *The Peacemaker* wants stability in life and inner peace.

Key Fear: The Peacemaker fears being separated from others. They also fear losing others too.

Wings possibilities: If you're able to adapt well to new ideas and encourage other people, you could be Enneagram type nine with an eight-wing, and this means you are *The Referee*. If you're fair, and can see the different sides to every situation and you have a desire to help others, you could have be type nine with one-wing and this means you are *The Dreamer*.

Nine with an eight-wing: If you have an eight-wing, you're *The Referee*. You are excellent at building connections and you lead in an effective way. You're adaptable to change and enjoy exploring new ideas. You are great at encouraging others, but you can assert yourself in a professional capacity. You can struggle to when it comes to handling conflict, so you try to avoid it if possible. When you are faced with conflict, you react, and can be seen as being blunt and awkward. If you learn how to manage conflict and use your assertiveness skills, you can overcome this barrier easily. It's all about maintaining the right balance for you (Enneagram Type 9w8 - The Advisor, 2020)[lix].

Nine with a one-wing: If you have a nine-wing, you're *The Dreamer.* That means you have a strong work ethic and you are motivated towards your purpose in life. You want to help others to improve and you assess every avenue before you make a judgement or decision. Your open mindedness makes you stand out, but sometimes you are overly critical of yourself. You struggle to face difficulties head on, but this is something you can improve if you build your assertiveness skills. (Enneagram Type 9w1 - The Negotiator, 2020)[lx].

Key motivations: Nines want nothing more than peace and harmony. They'll do anything to create that environment and they live to preserve this. They are attracted to stability and they resist anything that tries to prevent the smooth running of things.

Strengths: *The Peacemaker,* is devoted to the idea of peace and tranquility. They are harmonious in their work and life. They handle problems calmly and this helps everyone else around you calm too.

Nines have good instincts and a magnetic personality and they are powerful too. They are grounded and see the positive in everything.

Stress points and Growth:

As they move into the path of disintegration (stress) towards number 6, they become anxious and worried. Following the arrow of integration towards number 3 (growth), type Nines become interested in their own self-development and are often energetic (The Enneagram Institute, 2020)[lxi].

How *The Peacemaker* can hack their own success?

Of course, *The Peacemaker* will do anything to create harmony and peace, but they can use this to hack their own success. They are great listeners, mediators, and try their best not to upset others, which means they are great at reconciling others and dissolving conflicts. These are skills that you can hack for your own success:

- Use your search for harmony and your skills as a great listener to help others overcome barriers

and conflicts.
- Use your problem-solving techniques to overcome your own barriers but ensure you aren't too complacent.
- You are good at bringing people together, so use this skill, but work on your leadership skills to help you to inspire and lead others.
- Work on your assertiveness skills and build your confidence. You need to ensure your voice is heard. You have some valuable things to say, but you allow yourself to be overshadowed. It's time to be assertive and build your confidence.

Success goals are particularly important for nines, because you often overlook yourself and your own needs. You put yourself last because you prefer to ensure that everyone else around you is happy and at peace. Sometimes, we need to put ourselves first and goals will help you maintain focus. Think about success and what it means to you. Really consider how you can get there and what needs to be done. Write it all down and remind yourself of this everyday – once you've written down, you've committed to achieving these goals. You can do it!

Using the enneagram to achieve self-improvement

The Peacemaker is easy going and receptive to others. They are reassuring and are able to spread a sense of calm. You are very trusting and although this is a good trait, you are sometimes too trusting. You are also known to be stubborn and sometimes people see you as a pushover, because you like to avoid conflict and tension. You have the potential to flourish into a strong human being with excellent people and communitive skills. You just need to grow your confidence and be assertive when necessary.

If you're *The Peacemaker* you should:

- Work on your self-confidence. Sure, you like peace, but you can't let others take you for granted. Get in touch with your inner-self and tell it how strong you are. Believe it!
- Many people think of assertiveness as being a way to speak your mind and assert your authority. That's not always the same, and although you can assert authority, assertiveness

is about being able to say no, and the ability to instruct others clearly.

- Monitor your own feelings, thoughts and actions. You are known to go out of your way to avoid conflict, but sometimes this is something that we need to face head-on. Every time you are in danger of facing conflict or tension, but you manage to avoid it, note down the experience. Say *why you think you avoided it? What would happen if you faced it? Think about how you could handle it in an ideal world?* Exposure is a great way to start facing conflicts and tension – plan your exposure in advance so you're prepared ahead of time. Keep exposing yourself to situations that you would usually avoid, slowly. This will help you build your skills when it comes to dealing with such situations.

The Peacemaker may also need to work on their stubbornness too and ensure they don't confuse this with assertiveness. Always assess your actions objectively and consider whether you are being stubborn, or if you are making logical, objective decisions that will help you develop.

Strengthening Relationships – tapping into your own strengths

When it comes to personal and professional relationships, nines are supportive. They are very positive and patient when in a relationship together and often give others the benefit of the doubt when they do wrong. A nine is very forgiving and they are not afraid to show their emotion, and yet as they are a kindred spirit, they do not tend to make demands and pass judgement. You can really tell a nine anything!

The Peacemaker a great friend and a great colleague. They encourage others and love to try new things. They are creative and have a lot to contribute in a partnership as they are gentle and protective. They enjoy interaction and they are low maintenance as they are not concerned with anything materialistic.

Nines do not like tension or conflict, so they do everything in their power to avoid it, but this does not always solve the problem. They can become suppressive too, and occasionally, passive aggressive. They need to try and work on this part and face their conflicts. It's often best to talk about the difficult things in a relationship, as open and honest relationships last longer. Don't ignore those issues otherwise they will spiral.

Now, if nines want to strengthen their relationships, there are some things they/you can do:

- Ensure you are open and honest with the people who you are in a relationship with. This may mean that you have to grow your confidence.
- Talk about any problems. Don't bury your head in the sand and allow frustrations to fester.
- Use your qualities in staying calm and patient to enhance your relationship.
- Don't be afraid to have fun. Show your free-spirited side and show the other person in your relationship that you are spontaneous. Give them some attention!

To strengthen relationships, a nine should be themselves, but also ensure they don't let minor issues irritate them. They should work on their communication skills, as this will help them to build honest and open relationships that will last. A lot of your issues when it comes to a relationship stem from your lack of confidence, so keep working on this. You are generous, stable and steady, with a protective and caring temperament. You create positive relationships between colleagues, friends and families, and you can certainly strengthen them! (Relationship Type 9 with Type 9 — The Enneagram Institute, 2020)[lxii].

Achieving your career potential

There are many careers that would suit *The Peacemaker*. You prefer creative and caring roles on the whole because of your caring and free-spirited nature. You have many skills, like problem-solving skills, and you like to be around others, even though you don't always like to lead. You are a great listener, and although you're great at working in teams, sometimes you prefer to conduct your actual work role alone.

Nines make fantastic mediators or arbitrators because of their ability to facilitate problem-solving and you are skilled in overcoming barriers. They also have fantastic listening abilities, and this would serve you well in your role as a therapist or counsellor. Community work is also great for you as you are social and feel passionate about communities.

A nine longs to have a meaningful career and has a lot of skills and knowledge to share. They work best when they have something creative to do, and they like to use their thinking skills.

If you want to achieve your career potential, you need to ensure that you:

- Build your confidence in your career so you can get what you want and achieve any career goals.
- Find a career you're happy with. One that means a lot to you.
- Challenge yourself and push yourself. Start to build your communication and leadership skills.
- You're creative and this is something you can

use well to motivate others. It will make you a better colleague and help you to progress in the future.
- Ensure you do what you are good at – resolve problems and barriers, listen well, show care and empathy. Watch out for your stubborn side – work on that and don't let it take over. Use self-reflection to improve and grow.

To succeed in your career, think about the direction you want to head in:

- It's definitely important to work on a career plan. You probably don't have one, because you tend to simply take things as they come. Don't forget to add a personal development section and plan a way forward. *What skills and qualifications do you need to achieve your goal?*
- Use a reflective journal to make the most of your career. Think about what you might change or do. Ensure you list your career goals in the front of your book so you can review them everyday – sometimes nines need reminding.

Dig deep inside yourself and fine a career that you feel passionate about. You may enjoy working in the community, in social services, healthcare or education. Choose something that you personally find rewarding and you're destined to succeed (Enneagram Type 9 - The Peacemaker, 2020)[lxiii].

Master your finances by honing your skills

When it comes to finances, *The Peacemaker* is not always extremely organized. There are ways that they can develop and master your finances:

- You should know all incomings and outgoings if you want to master your finances. It's important to keep track of everything.
- Ensure you're realistic when it comes to money. Don't spend what you don't have, and ensure if you tie anything up in investments, you can afford this too. Make sure you have access to enough money to keep you going.
- Create a money mantra that suits you. Use questions or statements, for example, '*only buy*

what you need...' is a good mantra. What about setting yourself a budget too?

- If you have some money to invest, you should speak to a financial expert. Too often, people don't get the right advice, so go to a reputable firm. They might be able to save and grow your money.

The Peacemaker isn't very organised when it comes to money. They don't always consider how they use it, and sometimes they make mistakes with calculations, or overspend. This is due to the relationship they have with money. You need to do some mindset work, and rather than thinking you don't have money or you'll never have enough money, you need to start thinking about how you can make the money you need. It's time to take control of your money by changing your ideas of what you can and can't do when it comes to money. We actually block ourselves from earning our full potential. Money is just a number, and with your creative thinking skills, you have the power to grow and earn more, provided you don't block yourself. Concentrate on the *why* and the *how!*

Build emotional, mental, and physical health practices that work best for *The Peacemaker*

You have excellent emotional, mental and physical health typically, because you are so calm, avoid stress, and you take good care of yourself. Self-care is so important because it keeps your mind and body active.

Your physical health is something you often get distracted from. You prefer to work on quick activities that will get your heart racing and your mind active. Exercise eliminates stress:

- Swimming is a great exercise for you, because it's flexible. You can swim for a long or short time, it's down to you and how much time you can spare.
- Try some laughter yoga. If you don't take exercise to seriously, why not try some laughter yoga. We can all do with an extra laugh in our life. Try this and you won't be disappointed!

Generally, you're good at caring for your own mental

and emotional health. Your emotional and mental health is important to you and you're already in touch with your inner self. The main thing for you to work on is talking about the things that are on your mind and processing them effectively:

- Journaling is a great way for you to log your thoughts and feelings.
- When you feel frustrated about something, ensure that you talk to a friend, a family member, or there are even hotlines you can call to talk through your worries. These people are trained to deal with these types of things.
- You can use some breathing techniques or mediations to calm your mind. You can then self-reflect and assess situations before you act.

You should spend time each day working on your physical, emotional and mental health. Complete at least 30-minute exercise each day. It's also good to take some time for rest. Even if you just kickback for a while!

Become a Leadership Rockstar with your Enneagram skillset

The Peacemaker's strength does not always lie in their leadership skills. That's because other things are more important to them, such as caring for others, being compassionate, and embracing opportunities. The good thing is that you have many skills that mean you'll be a great leader. You just have to hone those further.

Nines can become great leaders if they:

- Work on your confidence. This will help you to polish any leadership skills and push you to be the best.
- Take your communication skills to the next level.
- Harness your listening skills and use them to coordinate your team. Take their opinions into account and respond accordingly.
- You've got good mediation, problem-solving and conflict resolution skills. You can use them when facilitating your team in their day to day activities. Lead by example and model these skills for your

team.
- Ensure you work on your organizational skills. You need these skills to improve your working methods and team management skills.

Leading isn't something you necessarily imagined yourself doing in your chosen career, but it is possible, and you could certainly do that well. Keep working on your skills and you'll make a fantastic leader.

Top Tips to Boost your efficiency through problem-solving methods that work for you

You're a natural problem solver. You are able to assess the pros and cons of a situation and resolve problems easily. You're good at listening and mediating to ensure barriers are overcome. You can facilitate this between people, and this is useful if you work in a team. You're determined to get to the bottom of the problem and figure it out.

You've got some excellent creative thinking skills and by using your logic, problem solving is efficient and effective for you. There is a chance you can improve your efficiency further, and to do this, you should:

- Listen to what others identify as being the problem and how to overcome it. Compare your ideas using brainstorming skills and weigh up your options.
- Ensure you keep communication channels open by being friendly and approachable. Use your kind and caring nature to ensure that everyone feels that they can contribute.
- Research problems and solutions. What are other people or businesses doing?
- Lead the problem-solving process, and keep people focused on identifying the problem and solution. This may mean using a problem-solving formula. If you hold a meeting when problem solving, you must reach an agreement amongst the attendees such that there's no such thing as a bad idea/question. Perhaps you can set a rule that everyone must contribute to the discussion. This will ensure you get maximum impact from your meeting.

Strong problem-solving techniques can make an impact and help you lead the way in your career and business.

Discover a path to spirituality that works best for your personality type

This is easy for *The Peacemaker,* as they are a very spiritual person. They enjoy reading their horoscopes, and healing using holistic therapies. They search their inner selves for answers and have a great sense of self-awareness which stems from their ability to meditate.

To improve your path to spirituality, you need to follow the things you believe in. If you are religious, then you can follow your path using your religious beliefs. Your Spirituality can help you:

- Grow and develop as a person.
- Find inner peace, which sets you up for outer peace.
- Can help you think clearly and reprogram your mind.

- Improve your listening and communication skills.

The Peacemaker can practice spirituality in many different ways. Things like meditation, mindfulness, and hypnotherapy are great ways to practice your spirituality. *What about tuning forks for to improve your outer energy?* Tuning forks can build your energy levels and help you become more productive, so if you have not done this already, be sure to try this holistic therapy.

Connect the dots to create a vision for progress and growth

Everyone needs a personal growth plan. If your dominant personality is *The Peacemaker,* it's time to create your vision. To connect the dots, we need to look at the 9 levels of development for this particular personality type. They will help you to choose your vision for the future, so you can recognize the healthy and unhealthy signs of your personality. You should always strive for healthy levels, 1-3. Average levels are 4-6, but if you find yourself dropping to level 6, you need to really focus on making steady improvements. If your levels are unhealthy (levels 7-9), action is needed now, and you may even need extra support from a medical professional. Remember it's important to monitor your levels.

Healthy levels

Level 1 – This is *The Peacemaker* at their very best and they can be fully connected to themselves and others. Spirituality means a lot and it factors into their contentment in life. They are fulfilled, and yet, have never felt more alive. They are truly happy and peaceful, both inside and out.

Level 2 – At level 2, *The Peacemaker* has a great nature and is very sincere. They accept others for who they are, and it doesn't affect them personally, because their emotions are under control. They feel ease with their life and selves, but they can be quite innocent and naïve too. Sometimes they put the trust in the wrong person, but mostly, they are receptive and attract positive people.

Level 3 – At level 3, *The Peacemaker* enjoys bringing

people together – it's one of their talents. They have strong communication skills and have a way of soothing others due to their optimism, and their reassuring and supportive nature. They are healers and can mediate awkward situations, well. They have a very calming nature, and this impacts others.

Average levels

Level 4 – At level 4, *The Peacemaker* sometimes falls into conventional roles. Sometimes they feel pressurized by the ideas and expectations of others, and they fear conflicts. They have idealized ideas and can start to be submissive by just doing what other people ask or tell them to do without question. They are accommodating, and if they don't know what to do, they are too ashamed to ask which puts their honesty in jeopardy.

Level 5 – *The Peacemaker* is disengaged. They've tuned out and separate themselves, focusing only on their problems and themselves. They bury their heads in the sand and are quite complacent when it comes to working as a team. Reading sometimes gives them a safe escape, as they would rather avoid problems than face them. Their problem-solving skills really start to suffer at this stage.

Level 6 – When at level 6, *The Peacemaker* pretends that problems aren't as bad as they sound. This is an attempt to save others the worry. They wish things were different but take no action. Their attention is often taken elsewhere which makes them feel angry. They wish they had a magic wand as they are not in the correct frame of mind for problem solving.

Unhealthy levels

Level 7 – *The Peacemaker* can start disassociating themselves from others and conflicts. They are neglectful and ineffectual and are not able to face their problems. They feel repressed, ignore problems, and avoid self-development, which is really what they need to lift their spirits and spark their motivation.

Level 8 – At this level, *The Peacemaker* has started to feel numb. They block out everything and anything and have lost all sense of awareness. They are unable to function properly and ignore the degree of self-awareness that they spent such a long time building up.

Level 9 – This is the lowest level and at level 9, *The Peacemaker* is very disorientated. They are unaware of what's going on around them and they have completely abandoned themselves. They could possibly have multiple personalities, or a personality disorder and they are catatonic. They really need assistance from a medical professional if they are to improve.

If you are *The Peacemaker,* self-awareness is key to your success! That's because everything is built on who you are, your nature and your spirituality. Ensure you spend time working on yourself, and don't get bogged down by what you can do for others. If people take advantage of you, it will get you down and you will start dipping to unhealthy levels. You're much more productive when you're at healthy levels. (The Enneagram Institute, 2020)[lxiv]

Affirmations for *The Peacemaker*

I am growing and changing as a person, for the better.

It's okay to say no.

I am strong but I'm still important. Self-care is for everyone and it helps me grow as a person.

CONCLUSION

The Enneagram is a great way to find out more about yourself, but it's a much broader topic than anticipated. This book is a great introduction and it has certainly explored what makes each personality tick, and what their strengths and desires are too. It has focused on helping you learn more about the Enneagram model and ideas, and the quiz has helped you conclude what personality type holds dominance within you. This book has therefore introduced you to the power of Enneagram and it's explained how you can harness that power to grow and reach your full potential. It would, however, be naïve to suggest that this book covers everything to do with Enneagram, because a book of that nature would be much larger.

The more the Enneagram is explored and understood, the more it has to offer. This book offers a taste but there are many books and much information out there that focus on one personality type, and some specifically in one area of that personality. There is so much information in books that looks at loving, sexual relationships that focus only on one relationship type, but this is a strict niche and the idea of a relationship is so much broader. A relationship can occur with our family, friends, colleagues, and professionally too. It's not always about who you're dating but maintaining positive relationships throughout our lives.

The psychology behind the Enneagram is useful as there is certainly evidence that confirms that knowing yourself and your own mind can ultimately help us to progress ourselves and our career. There are lots of books about *The Law of Attraction* and being able to manifest positivity in order to improve one's mindset, yet, with the Enneagram, although it also has a spiritual aspect, it focuses simply on knowing one's self and they way we react or think. It's about making those positive changes, based on what we know in relation to our personality, our needs, our fears and our desires. This is so we can maintain a healthy balance, stay motivated and to give us the tools so we can be the best that we can be. We make choices and decisions ourselves, so the Enneagram idea makes us accountable – it prompts us to take responsibility for our own actions. Being accountable and responsible is part of growing up and if the Enneagram reminds us of anything, it should be that we are adults and WE make the choices in our lives that shape our future.

As human beings, we tend to ignore the things about ourselves that we think to be negative. It's like we protect ourselves, and in some way, we deny it to ourselves (that's wasn't us...). The Enneagram personality types are honest, and they highlight when we are slipping into those unhealthy levels and with this imbalance being so detailed, it's hard for us to deny that we are spiralling. By giving us the tools we need to identify what's healthy for us and what isn't, we are more likely to maintain balance, or it even pushes us to strive for level 1 – the highest level, because we want to be the best that we can be. It's the knowledge it provides that prompts our own behavior, so we can strive to be the best.

It's important that we harness the power we are given throughout this book. That power comes through the form of knowledge and understanding, and yet, we all know that knowledge is power. Just remember, that when you've worked through this book, found out your personality type and you've started to make some changes, that this is just a taste of what the Enneagram model has to offer. There's more power at your fingertips and now we're passing on further responsibility and power to you because if you want more… If you really want to enhance the power of Enneagram further, then you must explore further. You know your personality type, but what about your centers and your wings? Have you really got to grips with these yet? If the answer is 'No!' then you should really move on right now and find out more. This book should've sparked a fire in you. It should've fired-up your motivation – so go out there and clasp what you want with both hands.

To conclude, it's important to remember that the power of Enneagram is now yours. Now is the time to use it!

REFERENCE LIST

[i] The Enneagram Institute. (2020). How The System Works — The Enneagram Institute. [online] Available at: https://www.enneagraminstitute.com/how-the-enneagram-system-works/ [Accessed 3 Apr. 2020].

[ii] Innercle.com. 2020. A Quick Guide To Wings In Enneagram - Innercle.Com. [online] Available at: <https://innercle.com/enneagram/a-quick-guide-to-wings-in-enneagram/> [Accessed 3 April 2020].

[iii] The Enneagram Institute. (2020). How The System Works — The Enneagram Institute. [online] Available at: https://www.enneagraminstitute.com/how-the-enneagram-system-works/ [Accessed 31 Jan. 2020].

[iv] Cloete, D. (2020). Origins and History of the Enneagram. [online] test. Available at: https://www.integrative9.com/enneagram/history/ [Accessed 10 Feb. 2020].

[v] Cloete, D. (2020). Origins and History of the Enneagram. [online] test. Available at: https://www.integrative9.com/enneagram/history/ [Accessed 12 Feb. 2020].

[vi] Art of wellbeing. (2020). How to Use the Enneagram of Personality for Personal Growth. [online] Available at: http://www.artofwellbeing.com/2017/11/01/enneagramofpersonality/ [Accessed 10 Feb. 2020].

[vii] Art of wellbeing. (2020). How to Use the Enneagram of Personality for Personal Growth. [online] Available at: http://www.artofwellbeing.com/2017/11/01/enneagramofpersonality/ [Accessed 10 Feb. 2020].

[viii] The Enneagram Institute. (2020). Type One — The Enneagram Institute. [online] Available at: https://www.enneagraminstitute.com/type-1 [Accessed 11 Feb. 2020].

[ix] Crystalknows.com. 2020. Enneagram Type 1W2 - The Activist. [online] Available at: < Crystalknows.com. 2020. Enneagram Type 1W9 - The Individualist. [online] Available at: < https://www.crystalknows.com/enneagram/type-1-wing-9> [Accessed 3 April 2020].

[x] Crystalknows.com. 2020. Enneagram Type 1W2 - The Activist. [online] Available at: <https://www.crystalknows.com/enneagram/type-1-wing-2> [Accessed 3 April 2020].

[xi] The Enneagram Institute. (2020). Type One — The Enneagram Institute. [online] Available at: https://www.enneagraminstitute.com/type-1 [Accessed 11 Feb. 2020].
[xii] May Busch Crystalknows.com. 2020. Enneagram Type 1W2 - The Activist. [online] Available at: <https://www.crystalknows.com/enneagram/type-1-wing-2> [Accessed 3 April 2020].. (2020). 8 Ways to Stop Being a Perfectionist | May Busch. [online] Available at: https://maybusch.com/8-ways-stop-being-perfectionist/ [Accessed 11 Feb. 2020].
[xiii] The Enneagram Institute. 2020. Relationship Type 1 With Type 1 — The Enneagram Institute. [online] Available at: <https://www.enneagraminstitute.com/relationship-type-1-with-type-1> [Accessed 24 March 2020].
[xiv] Crystalknows.com. 2020. Enneagram Type 1 - The Idealist. [online] Available at: <https://www.crystalknows.com/enneagram/type-1> [Accessed 24 March 2020].
[xv] The Enneagram Institute. (2020). Type One — The Enneagram Institute. [online] Available at: https://www.enneagraminstitute.com/type-1 [Accessed 11 Feb. 2020].
[xvi] The Enneagram Institute. (2020). Type Two — The Enneagram Institute. [online] Available at: https://www.enneagraminstitute.com/type-2/ [Accessed 16 Feb. 2020].
[xvii] Crystalknows.com. 2020. Enneagram Type 2W1 - The Companion. [online] Available at: <https://www.crystalknows.com/enneagram/type-2-wing-1> [Accessed 3 April 2020].
[xviii] Crystalknows.com. 2020. Enneagram Type 2W3 - The Host. [online] Available at: <https://www.crystalknows.com/enneagram/type-2-wing-3> [Accessed 3 April 2020].
[xix] The Enneagram Institute. (2020). Type Two — The Enneagram Institute. [online] Available at: https://www.enneagraminstitute.com/type-2/ [Accessed 16 Feb. 2020].
[xx] The Enneagram Institute. 2020. Relationship Type 2 With Type 2 — The Enneagram Institute. [online] Available at: < https://www.enneagraminstitute.com/relationship-type-2-with-type-2> [Accessed 24 March 2020].
[xxi] Crystalknows.com. 2020. Enneagram Type 2 – The Caregiver. [online] Available at: <https://www.crystalknows.com/enneagram/type-2> [Accessed 24 March 2020].
[xxii] The Enneagram Institute. (2020). Type Two — The Ennea-

gram Institute. [online] Available at: https://www.enneagraminstitute.com/type-2/ [Accessed 19 Feb. 2020].

[xxiii] Crystalknows.com. 2020. Enneagram Type 3 wing 2 – The Enchanter. [online] Available at: < https://www.crystalknows.com/enneagram/type-3-wing-2> [Accessed 4 April 2020]

[xxiv] Crystalknows.com. 2020. Enneagram Type 3 wing 4 – The Expert. [online] Available at: < https://www.crystalknows.com/enneagram/type-3-wing-4 [Accessed 4 April 2020)

[xxv] The Enneagram Institute. (2020). Type Three — The Enneagram Institute. [online] Available at: https://www.enneagraminstitute.com/type-3/ [Accessed 21 Feb. 2020].

[xxvi] The Enneagram Institute. 2020. Relationship Type 3 With Type 3 — The Enneagram Institute. [online] Available at: <https://www.enneagraminstitute.com/relationship-type-3-with-type-3> [Accessed 24 March 2020].

[xxvii] Crystalknows.com. 2020. Enneagram Type 3 – The Performer. [online] Available at: <https://www.crystalknows.com/enneagram/type-3> [Accessed 24 March 2020].

[xxviii] The Enneagram Institute. (2020). Type Two — The Enneagram Institute. [online] Available at:

[xxix] The Enneagram Institute. (2020). Type Three — The Enneagram Institute. [online] Available at: https://www.enneagraminstitute.com/type-3/ [Accessed 21 Feb. 2020].

[xxx] Crystalknows.com. 2020. Enneagram Type 4 wing 3 – The Enthusiast. [online] Available at: < https://www.crystalknows.com/enneagram/type-4-wing-3 [Accessed 4 April 2020)

[xxxi] Crystalknows.com. 2020. Enneagram Type 4 wing 3 – The Free Spirit. [online] Available at: < https://www.crystalknows.com/enneagram/type-4-wing-5 [Accessed 4 April 2020)

[xxxii] The Enneagram Institute. (2020). Type Four— The Enneagram Institute. [online] Available at: https://www.enneagraminstitute.com/type-4/ [Accessed 21 Feb. 2020]

[xxxiii] The Enneagram Institute. 2020. Relationship Type 4 With Type 4 — The Enneagram Institute. [online] Available at: <https://www.enneagraminstitute.com/relationship-type-4-with-type-4> [Accessed 24 March 2020].

[xxxiv] Crystalknows.com. 2020. Enneagram Type 4 - The Creative. [online] Available at: <https://www.crystalknows.com/ennea-

gram/type-4> [Accessed 24 March 2020].
[xxxv] The Enneagram Institute. (2020). Type Four— The Enneagram Institute. [online] Available at: https://www.enneagraminstitute.com/type-4/ [Accessed 21 Feb. 2020].
[xxxvi] Crystalknows.com. 2020. Enneagram Type 5 wing 4 – The Philosopher. [online] Available at: < https://www.crystalknows.com/enneagram/type-5-wing-4 [Accessed 4 April 2020)
[xxxvii] Crystalknows.com. 2020. Enneagram Type 5 wing 6 – The Troubleshooter. [online] Available at: < https://www.crystalknows.com/enneagram/type-5-wing-6 [Accessed 4 April 2020)
[xxxviii] The Enneagram Institute. (2020). Type Five— The Enneagram Institute. [online] Available at: https://www.enneagraminstitute.com/type-5/ [Accessed 21 Feb. 2020].
[xxxix] The Enneagram Institute. 2020. Relationship Type 5 With Type 5 — The Enneagram Institute. [online] Available at: <https://www.enneagraminstitute.com/relationship-type-5-with-type-5> [Accessed 24 March 2020].
[xl] Crystalknows.com. 2020. Enneagram Type 5 - The Thinker. [online] Available at: <https://www.crystalknows.com/enneagram/type-5> [Accessed 24 March 2020].
[xli] The Enneagram Institute. (2020). Type Five— The Enneagram Institute. [online] Available at: https://www.enneagraminstitute.com/type-5/ [Accessed 21 Feb. 2020].
[xlii] Crystalknows.com. 2020. Enneagram Type 6 wing 5 – The Guardian. [online] Available at: < https://www.crystalknows.com/enneagram/type-6-wing-5 [Accessed 4 April 2020)
[xliii] Crystalknows.com. 2020. Enneagram Type 6 wing 7 – The Confidant. [online] Available at: < https://www.crystalknows.com/enneagram/type-6-wing-7 [Accessed 4 April 2020)
[xliv] The Enneagram Institute. (2020). Type Six— The Enneagram Institute. [online] Available at: https://www.enneagraminstitute.com/type-6/ [Accessed 21 Feb. 2020].
[xlv] The Enneagram Institute. 2020. Relationship Type 6 With Type 6 — The Enneagram Institute. [online] Available at: <https://www.enneagraminstitute.com/relationship-type-6-with-type-6> [Accessed 24 March 2020].

[xlvi] Crystalknows.com. 2020. Enneagram Type 6 - The Loyalist. [online] Available at: <https://www.crystalknows.com/enneagram/type-6> [Accessed 24 March 2020].
[xlvii] The Enneagram Institute. (2020). Type Six — The Enneagram Institute. [online] Available at: https://www.enneagraminstitute.com/type-6/ [Accessed 21 Feb. 2020].
[xlviii] Crystalknows.com. 2020. Enneagram Type 7 wing 6 – The Pathfinder. [online] Available at: < https://www.crystalknows.com/enneagram/type-7-wing-6 [Accessed 4 April 2020)
[xlix] Crystalknows.com. 2020. Enneagram Type 7 wing 8 – The Opportunist. [online] Available at: < https://www.crystalknows.com/enneagram/type-7-wing-8 [Accessed 4 April 2020)
[l] The Enneagram Institute. (2020). Type Seven— The Enneagram Institute. [online] Available at: https://www.enneagraminstitute.com/type-7/ [Accessed 21 Feb. 2020].
[li] The Enneagram Institute. 2020. Relationship Type 7 With Type 7 — The Enneagram Institute. [online] Available at: <https://www.enneagraminstitute.com/relationship-type-7-with-type-7> [Accessed 24 March 2020].
[lii] Crystalknows.com. 2020. Enneagram Type 7 - The Adventurer. [online] Available at: <https://www.crystalknows.com/enneagram/type-7> [Accessed 24 March 2020].
[liii] The Enneagram Institute. (2020). Type Seven— The Enneagram Institute. [online] Available at: https://www.enneagraminstitute.com/type-7/ [Accessed 21 Feb. 2020].
[liv] Crystalknows.com. 2020. Enneagram Type 8 wing 7 – The Nonconformist. [online] Available at: < https://www.crystalknows.com/enneagram/type-8-wing-7 [Accessed 4 April 2020)
[lv] Crystalknows.com. 2020. Enneagram Type 8 wing 9 – The Diplomat. [online] Available at: < https://www.crystalknows.com/enneagram/type-8-wing-9 [Accessed 4 April 2020)
[lvi] The Enneagram Institute. (2020). Type Eight— The Enneagram Institute. [online] Available at: https://www.enneagraminstitute.com/type-8/ [Accessed 21 Feb. 2020].
[lvii] The Enneagram Institute. 2020. Relationship Type 8 With Type81 — The Enneagram Institute. [online] Available at: <https://www.enneagraminstitute.com/relationship-type-8-with-type-8> [Accessed 24 March 2020].

[lviii] Crystalknows.com. 2020. Enneagram Type 8 - The Protector. [online] Available at: <https://www.crystalknows.com/enneagram/type-8> [Accessed 24 March 2020].
[lix] The Enneagram Institute. (2020). Type Eight— The Enneagram Institute. [online] Available at: https://www.enneagraminstitute.com/type-8/ [Accessed 21 Feb. 2020].
[lx] Crystalknows.com. 2020. Enneagram Type 9 wing 8 – The Advisor. [online] Available at: < https://www.crystalknows.com/enneagram/type-9-wing-8 [Accessed 4 April 2020)
[lxi] Crystalknows.com. 2020. Enneagram Type 9 wing 1 – The Negotiator. [online] Available at: < https://www.crystalknows.com/enneagram/type-9-wing-1 [Accessed 4 April 2020)
[lxii] The Enneagram Institute. (2020). Type Nine— The Enneagram Institute. [online] Available at: https://www.enneagraminstitute.com/type-9/ [Accessed 21 Feb. 2020].
[lxiii] The Enneagram Institute. 2020. Relationship Type 9 With Type 9 — The Enneagram Institute. [online] Available at: <https://www.enneagraminstitute.com/relationship-type-9-with-type-9> [Accessed 24 March 2020].
[lxiv] Crystalknows.com. 2020. Enneagram Type 9 - The Peacemaker. [online] Available at: <https://www.crystalknows.com/enneagram/type-9> [Accessed 24 March 2020].
[lxv] The Enneagram Institute. (2020). Type Nine— The Enneagram Institute. [online] Available at: https://www.enneagraminstitute.com/type-9/ [Accessed 21 Feb. 2020].

www.ingramcontent.com/pod-product-compliance
Lightning Source LLC
Chambersburg PA
CBHW020901080526
44589CB00011B/390